John Muir Trail Country

GUIDE TO THE HIGH SIERRA

JOHN MUIR TRAIL
PACIFIC CREST TRAIL (Lower Kern to Sonora Pass Road)
SIERRA FOREST TRAIL (Sequoia to Yosemite)
HIGH SIERRA TRAIL (Sequoia to Mt. Whitney)
East and West Entry Points

FAMILY CAMPERS

BACKPACKERS   FISHERMEN

John Muir Trail Country

LEW AND GINNY CLARK

A Western Trails Publication

My trail is the wilderness trail
Tho trod before by a thousand feet
It is new to me.
A venture to discover new ways
To explore secrets of nature
And questions of the mind
That become lost
In the sea of humanity and time.

Revised Edition, Second Printing, 1978
Library of Congress Number 76-53247
ISBN 0-931532-02-7
Western Trails Publication
Box 2637, Escondido, California 92025

In this book on the Muir Trail, you'll find a guide which will take you along one of the best known trails in the country. It should not be used in the way of a road map, but more appropriately as a reference to learn about the area and its native inhabitants and to stimulate thoughts of our natural resources; thoughts of yesterdays, today, and all the tomorrows. Hopefully, those who will some day follow our footsteps along this trail will appreciate the gentle care, concern, and respect which you've shown for our God-given natural heritage, and they, in turn, will repay in kind.

What better place to realize what John Muir wrote so long ago:

"Climb the mountains and get their good tidings;
Nature's peace will flow into you as sunshine
into flowers;
The winds will blow their freshness into you and
the storms their energy, and cares will drop off
like autumn leaves."

Sierra

Trails

STANLEY T. ALBRIGHT
Associate Regional Director
Operations, Western Region
National Park Service

The John Muir Trail, a monument to the memory of a famed American naturalist and explorer of the Sierra, links Mt. Whitney on the south to Tuolumne Meadows in Yosemite National Park.

The trail traverses much of the crest of John Muir's beloved Sierra Nevada Range and runs for 184 miles through the spectacular back country of the Inyo National Forest and adjoining Sequoia and Kings Canyon National Parks, Sierra National Forest, and Yosemite National Park.

I can imagine no better way for a person to get "in touch" with himself and with his heritage then to trek a portion, or all, of this trail. The beauty and solitude is unsurpassed.

It is there for you to enjoy. Do so, and leave it as unspoiled and beautiful as you would like to find it.

ROBERT L. RICE
Forest Supervisor
Inyo National Forest

Contents

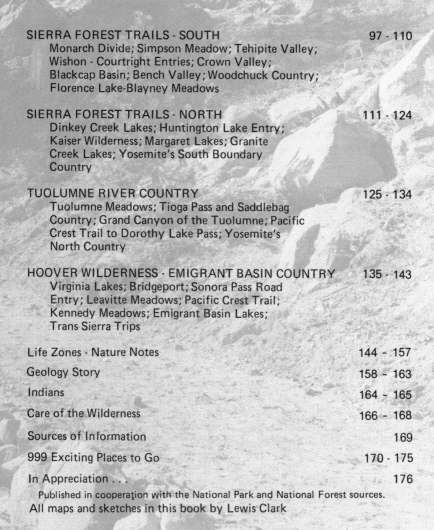

Published in cooperation with the National Park and National Forest sources.
All maps and sketches in this book by Lewis Clark

Trails

of

John Muir

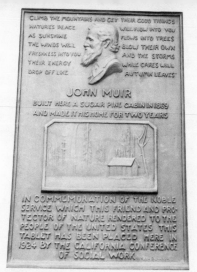

"CLIMB THE MOUNTAINS AND GET THEIR GOOD TIDINGS
NATURE'S PEACE WILL FLOW INTO YOU
AS SUNSHINE FLOWS INTO TREES
THE WINDS WILL BLOW THEIR OWN
FRESHNESS INTO YOU AND THE STORMS
THEIR ENERGY WHILE CARES WILL
DROP OFF LIKE AUTUMN LEAVES"

JOHN MUIR
BUILT HERE A SUGAR PINE CABIN IN 1869
AND MADE IT HIS HOME FOR TWO YEARS

IN COMMEMORATION OF THE NOBLE
SERVICE WHICH THIS FRIEND AND PRO-
TECTOR OF NATURE RENDERED TO THE
PEOPLE OF THE UNITED STATES THIS
TABLET HAS BEEN PLACED HERE IN
1924 BY THE CALIFORNIA CONFERENCE
OF SOCIAL WORK

Completely at peace with man and nature he ventured unafraid with both. The outdoors was his laboratory for research and temple of worship. People found in him a way of life they had sought but never had the time to experience.

An Emigrant of Life, he had entered it in Scotland, paused a while in mid-eastern America while nature changed him from a child into a youth, then pressed on to venture with nature which completely absorbed him as a way of life. His very name, Muir, was a projection of the Scottish word meaning the wild, open "moor".

The notes of his ramblings, intense in accuracy interpreting the land and its living things, were akin to a religious hymn of reverence, joy, and thanksgiving for having been a part of this great emigration.

He ran breathless through life as if afraid it would end before he had a chance to experience it all. His encounters in addition to the Sierra included the Alps, Himalayas, and the Amazon. By canoe with Indians, he explored the Alaska glacier later to bear his name.

Disregarding season and difficulty he made the mountains his home. In seeking answers to what forces of nature wrought the yosemites of the Sierra he followed the rivers through desperate canyon gorges to their fountainheads in drops of water gathering at more than three-score glaciers along its skyline crests.

A guide to Ralph Waldo Emerson in the giant Sequoias, a camping companion to Theodore Roosevelt in the Yosemite, a researcher with university scientists, and a fellow-worker with shepherds at the high meadows of Tuolumne, he explored the range of life as he roamed his *Range of Light* and left in his notes and associations that spirit of enjoyment that included sharing it with others. His milestones in living became trail-markers in his emigration through life.

What other name than that of John Muir could have been given the great Sierra crest trail? Truly the odyssey of an emigrant experiencing life as he lived it to its fullest.

"... the trail to be constructed ... shall be known as the JOHN MUIR TRAIL in honor of the late John Muir who has performed an inestimable service in making known to the world the wonders of the mountains of California."
(Signed) Governor Hiram Johnson Governor, State of California -- May 17, 1915

JOHN MUIR — MAN OF THE WILDERNESS

(Mileposts In The Life of An Emigrant)

1838 Birth (Apr. 28) Dunbar, Scotland.

1849 Sailed from Glasco, Scotland, to U.S. Family settled in Wisconsin.

1860 Displayed inventions at Wisconsin State Fair.

1861-63 Attended University of Wisconsin. Studies geology, biology.

1866-67 Wheelwright in wagon-wheel factory, Indianapolis.

1867 Eye injury. Resolve to see all he could. Upon recovery, began his 1,000 mile walk to the Gulf of Mexico.

1868 Sailed to Cuba seeking passage to South America. Back to New York. Then to California to see the Yosemite. Visit to Yosemite confirmed his resolve to explore it further. Worked in San Joaquin Valley for winter.

1869 Assumed job as custodian of 2,000 sheep and shepherds for season in Tuolumne Meadows. Worked winters for Hutchins in a sawmill in Yosemite, some five years. Explorations and conclusions about Yosemite's formation contrary to Whitney's.

1870 Le Conte's visit to Yosemite. Excursion of U.C. students included Tenaya Lake, Tuolumne Meadows, Mono Lake. Muir's premise on glacial formation accepted by Le Conte. Resolved to look for living glaciers to support premise.

1872 Ritter Peak ascent. Evidence of glacier. Led Geodetic Survey party to summit Mt. Shasta. Back to Yosemite. (Year of great earthquake.)

1873 Last year of established residence in Yosemite. Over six year period found 65 glaciers in High Sierra. Explored headwaters of San Joaquin, Kings, and Kaweah rivers.

1874 Explored headwaters of Feather and Yuba rivers. Guide to Geodetic Survey Party to Mt. Shasta. A second ascent with a friend later in year.

1875 Explored extent of sequoia groves between Yosemite and Sequoia. Made two ascents of Shasta.

1877 Ascent of Mt. Shasta with Asa Gray and Sir John Hooker. Followed by float trip 250 miles in homemade boat down Merced River

1878 Accompanied Geodetic Survey Party to highlands of Nevada and Great Basin country.

1879 Trip to Alaska. Explored Glacier Bay, Muir Glacier with Indian cancemen.

1880 Second Alaska trip. Continued glacier studies. "Stickeen" story.

1881 Third Alaska trip. Wrangel Island, Bering Sea, mouth of Yukon River. Upon return; marriage to Loui Wanda Stenzel. (Martinez) Operated fruit ranch for several years with father-in-law.

1890 Great project urging saving of trees and mountain areas completed with passage of acts setting aside Yosemite, Sequoia, and Gen. Grant Grove. U.S. Cavalry in charge at Yosemite. The "locusts" began their retreat from the high meadows. Need for organized support seen.

1892 Sierra Club founded. Muir first president.

1893 First book "The Mountains of California."

1897 Univ. Wisconsin granted Hon. Degree of LLD (Later by Yale, Harvard, and Univ. California).

1903 With Theodore Roosevelt to Yosemite. Camped out at Mariposa Grove, Glacier Point, and Yosemite Valley. Followed by establishment of 16 National Monuments. Doubled number of Nat'l Parks.

1908 Harriman's guest at Klamath Lake (Oregon). 1,000 pages notes on Muir's commentaries compiled. Visit to So. Am.: Rio De Janiero, Santos, Buenos Aires, then to Cape Town; Europe; Siberia; Manchuria; China; India; voyage up Nile; and Australia.)Wrote Roosevelt regarding Petrified Forest needing protection.)

1911 To So. America to see the noble trees of the Amazon.

1914 Death of Muir: Christmas Eve. Was reviewing notes on his last love and next book on Alaska travels. Part of the "glorious aurora of the Far North."

EARLY VISITORS

The building of the John Muir Trail was the outcome of needs and dreams of many people over a period of many years. It was a culmination of plans and existing trails that grew out of travel in the high mountains of California. Indians, following game from place to place, had developed routes that followed the most practical passes over the mountains. Early pathfinders of the West and later, the prospectors, followed many of the ancient trails and began developing others as needs arose. Stockmen extended these to move their sheep and cattle into the high mountain meadows as waves of settlers began to pre-empt the low valley grasslands.

Visits and explorations of the entire Sierra increased after 1870. The writings of John Muir extolled far and wide "the glorious wonders of the mountains of California." Government surveys were made, such as those of Joseph Whitney, to fill in the open spaces on the maps of the West. Scientists from the Smithsonian Institute built a stone hut on the summit of Mt. Whitney in 1909 to shelter men and equipment studying the sun's rays.

Scientists from the staffs of Stanford University and the University of California began conducting field trips into the Yosemite region. Foremost among these was Joseph LeConte whose unending studies of the mountains contributed much to their exploration and understanding.

The Sierra Club, founded in 1892, with John Muir as its president, began a campaign of exploration and conservation action by state and national legislators to preserve the integrity of the wilderness between the Yosemite and Mt. Whitney-Sequoia regions. Outings were conducted by the Club in 1901 to the Yosemite high country, in 1902 to the Kings River watershed, and in 1903 to the upper Kern River basin. Such visitations and their inevitable writings of the mountains soon advertised the backcountry Sierra to many eastern visitors including President Theodore Roosevelt. In 1903 he camped with Muir at Mariposa Grove, Glacier Point, and Yosemite Valley.

Such interest soon brought about the establishment of a plan of action for a controlled use and conservation of our natural resources. No longer could stockmen, miners, and lumbermen engage in the wanton destruction of the choice areas of the mountains. Placed under the management of the National Forest Service, guidelines were set up to insure use without abuse. Trails were built, maintained, and patrolled to supervise the regions assigned them.

National parks were created to protect special areas such as Sequoia and General Grant in 1890 and Yosemite in 1902. These were to become "museums of the great outdoors" and were to be kept as near as possible in their natural state. Sheep could no longer ravage flower filled meadows and a halt was called to the felling of giant sequoias to be split up for fence posts. Rangers and Naturalists were given the responsibility of the preservation and interpretation of these special areas. It was only a matter of time until the demand arose for a continuous trail along the crest of Muir's *Range of Light.*

DREAM OF A TRAIL

Early backcountry visitors included such men as Theodore Solomons who had long dreamed of such a trail. His first trip in 1892 explored the basins of the Merced, Tuolumne, and San Joaquin rivers. In 1894-95 he was back again seeking out the unexplored basins of the upper San Joaquin and headwaters of the Kings River.

Bolton Brown, a young Fine Arts professor at Stanford University began, in 1895, a series of wilderness adventures that included the headwaters of the Middle and South Forks of the Kings and upper Kern rivers. His drawings, maps, and reports provided definition and character of the regions visited.

Joseph LeConte, who had made repeated trips into the high country since his first explorations with Muir in 1870 now turned south. In 1898 he followed the routes of Solomons. In 1903 he was in the Palisades recording measurements of peaks and basins, In 1904 and 1906 he inspected the Goddard Divide region and speculated upon the prospects of a high country trail running the length of the Sierra between Yosemite and Sequoia national parks.

A DREAM BECOMES A REALITY

As attack after attack was made upon the unknown areas, LeConte became the more determined to complete the scouting of such a route. Early in the summer of 1908 he set out from Yosemite with two companions. After some four strenuous weeks they had covered almost three hundred miles of what was to become the general way of going of the proposed trail. Returning to their homes in the San Francisco Bay Area their findings and efforts, enjoined with many others, culminated in the passage of the state legislature bill providing authorization and funds for preliminary planning and construction. Work began under the supervision of the Park Service in Yosemite and Sequoia and by the Forest Service in the much larger, undeveloped area laying between the two parks.

Well experienced in this line of work the Forest Service people, with great enthusiasm, soon had the project under way. Two 8-man crews were put to work. One was at the Muir Pass section, the other on the upper Middle Fork of the Kings River.

Specifications and work on the trail insured its safe use. It was to be 30" in width with passing turnouts at dangerous places. Effort was made so its grade did not exceed 15%, that it avoided boggy meadows and slide areas, and was well identified with markers such as monuments, ducks, and tree-blazes to guide the visitor. Several bridges were built spanning the most troublesome rivers.

By the close of the 1916 season a passable trail had been completed. Since then, continued improvements have been made in route, grade, and signs. Access trails from the valleys to both east and west sides have increased from a half-dozen to 25 or 30 routes. From Happy Isles at the upper end of Yosemite Valley to Whitney Portal it covers approximately 225 miles and traverses the heart of some 7,000 square miles of scenic Sierra grandeur.

A Landscape Was Formed

Mt. Whitney from the North
Eugene Rose

The formation of the Sierra was due to a combination of many forces such as erosion, glacial action, and faulting. There is good evidence to support the premise that this was not a single, continuous action but rather a series of weather changes and faulting efforts spread over a long period of time. Also, there was undoubtedly, intermittent down-faulting action in the basin area to the east. Tremendous forces of nature were at work during these times. Only 80 miles to the east lies the Death Valley sink with its submerged floor more than 1,200' below sea level. Lying adjacent to it is Telescope Peak some 11,045' above sea level.

The mountains we see today are in geologic time, relatively young. Ages before them stood a cordillera running in a N-W by S-E pattern. Over millions of years the gigantic forces eventually broke down and carried away much of the material of these mountains depositing them in what is now the Great Central Valley of California. Not all of the old mountains were carried away. Many areas stood like unreal islands in a vast sea of ice. In the middle Sierra, sections of old materials remain unglaciated such as those in the Ritter-Banner area. Other ancient, towering peaks now long gone, left behind them rounded, almost flat-topped foothills from the Muir Crest on the south to the Kuna Crest on the north.

Repeated uplifts and neighboring down-faulting action contributed to the removal of the ancient mountains and replaced them with the towering granite rampart we find today. As the deep seated block began its gradual rise along its eastern front, waters of the old drainage routes began to cut deeper and deeper until obstructions and/or weakened sections along the lower ranges gave way causing a spill-through to the west. These waters began developing V-shaped canyons. Combining with other streams on the San Joaquin flood-plain they began their journey northward some 125 miles to the Pacific. Joining with waters from the Sacramento Valley their combined strength forced their way through the Coast range barrier and emptied into the Pacific, first at Monterey Bay, then as its distorted mouth became filled with sedimentary debris, broke through the last parallel barrier of the cordillera system at San Francisco's Golden Gate.

DIMENSIONS OF THE SIERRA

The over-all Sierra block is some 400 miles long and varies from 35 to 80 miles wide covering an area of more than 20,000 square miles. Most of it is between 3,000' and 10,000' elevation and supports life zones ranging from desert to alpine. It is a single, massive block so tilted that it slopes gently to the west from 14,000' along its crest to less than 100' in the Great Central Valley. Its east face presents a bold, aggressive, frontal escarpment rising an abrupt 10,000' above the Owens Valley. Its total dimensions make it higher, wider, and more spectacular than any other mountain range in the United States.

Twice the length of the Rocky Mountains, it stands 4,000' higher above its adjacent valleys than the Rockies do above the Great Plains. Pioneers found this formidable 7,000' barrier a final challenge on their westward trek. Today's visitors enjoy a top of the world experience crossing the Sierra at Tioga Pass at 9,941' with 12-13,000' peaks surrounding them. From there it is 180 miles south before a vehicular crossing at Walker's Pass is possible.

Upon the face of this vast block lies a series of lesser ranges lying in a general north-west to south-east pattern. Most of these would present a bulk of adequate dimension to warrant considerable attention if put into settings by themselves. In the south, the Great Western Divide separates the Kern-Kaweah basins. Its over 12,000' crest is often mistaken by Giant Forest visitors for the main crest of the Sierra which actually lies 14 miles farther east and is 2,500' higher. North of this lies the LeConte-White Divide and Kaiser Ridge separating the Kings and San Joaquin rivers. In the heart of the Yosemite lies the 25 miles long Cathedral-Ritter Range that includes a score of named and unnamed peaks above 10,000'. All of these minor ranges stand a good 2,500' to 4,000' above their surrounding valley floors. Along the main Sierra range is found 285 peaks over 12,000', 140 over 13,000' and 11 above 14,000'.

More than a dozen master streams carry the waters of this giant, westward tilted monolith down into the Central Valley. North of the Yosemite are the Feather, Yuba, Mokelumne, and Stanislaus rivers. In Yosemite the most outstanding valleys carry the waters of the Tuolumne and Merced Rivers. The Muir Gorge of the Tuolumne is a narrow mile deep trench with almost sheer granite walls. The waters of the San Joaquin carry the melting snows from the main basin and tributaries covering almost a thousand miles.

The deepest of the Sierra canyons lie in the heart of the Kings Canyon-Sequoia country. Here the roaring, tumbling streams are enclosed in great granite basins some 5,000' to 7,000' below their surrounding crests. Into the deepest canyons tumbling cascades and freefalling waters from hanging valleys add their beauty to the wild array.

Sierra Seasons

General weather conditions peculiar to the Sierra greatly influence its forest cover and wildlife. Its great height and slope to the west ensures the capture of the lions share of precipitation moving inland from the Pacific. Most of this falls during the winter months as snow. Converse to many regions, the greatest depths are deposited at the lower elevations — 5,000' to 6,000' and packs run between 30' to 60'. On Mt. Whitney, it averages 3' to 5', is very dry, and the prevailing winds soon blow it away — sometimes in great "snow banners", From the high Sierra peaks they drift far out and over the eastern valleys and plateaus. This contributes to the continuance of some three score glaciers and glacierettes hugging the north slopes of the larger peaks.

Summer brings little rain and what it does provide usually comes in the form of afternoon showers of short duration with clearing skies by evening. With only infrequent storms, and in general a very open forest with little undercover at the higher elevations, camping conditions are ideal.

This very advantage in camping conditions makes the Sierra more popular for a longer part of the year. Each season has its special attractions. Spring is crisp and glorious with the red bud in bloom, waterfalls at their best, and the mountain renewal, shimmering with alertness. Autumn colors, including the red-leaved dogwoods against the redwood bark of the sequoias, its striking, multi-colored leaves mixed with the deep green firs and pines throughout the forest, golden aspen along the meadow rims, squirrels running around scurrying for cones, the sharpness and briskness in the air as if the mountains were in their last burst of enthusiasm before accepting the coming snows — all make for a different mountain experience.

Fierce storms of short duration in some years are interspersed by many days of clear skies, and temperatures seldom below 20 degrees. Cross country trips have become more numerous by the ski touring enthusiasts. New ventures into the Sierra are opening for the hardy, experienced skier

A magnificient story has been written about the experience of Orland Bartholomew* who set out alone on Christmas Day in 1928 at the bottom of Cottonwood Canyon, south of Mt. Whitney. Following along the same general route as the John Muir Trail, he arrived in Yosemite Valley on April 3, 1929. During the late summer and fall he had surveyed the route and placed some eleven caches of food along the way. The diary of his experience reveal many unusual aspects of Sierra winters. He was very fortunate to have had a relatively open winter. In fact, some of the last sections of his journey he was reduced to walking and packing his skis.

Wildlife in such regions, set him a good example. Hole up during a storm, carry on during clear days! His companions included coyotes, wolverines, porcupines, water ouzels, Sierra hare, pine martens, and a wolf. In a number of places streams were flowing and he supplemented his diet with fresh trout. Bart's fourteen week venture included forty-two nights above 10,000' with temperatures as low as a minus 14 degrees. His three hundred mile journey provides an unusual picture of one Sierra winter mountaineering conditions, and most important, the quality of those who developed a true compatability with nature in the high country.

14   *HIGH ODYSSEY by Eugene A. Rose, Howell-North, 1050 Parker Street, Berkeley, Calif. 94710

by Orland Bartholomew at Muir Pass, February 1928

Sherman Tree   Bill Jones, NPS, Sequoia

Tiger Lily
Western Azalia
White Mariposa

Lupine
Marsh Marigold
Pine Violets

California Pink
Ground Rose
Cow Parsnips in Round Meadow

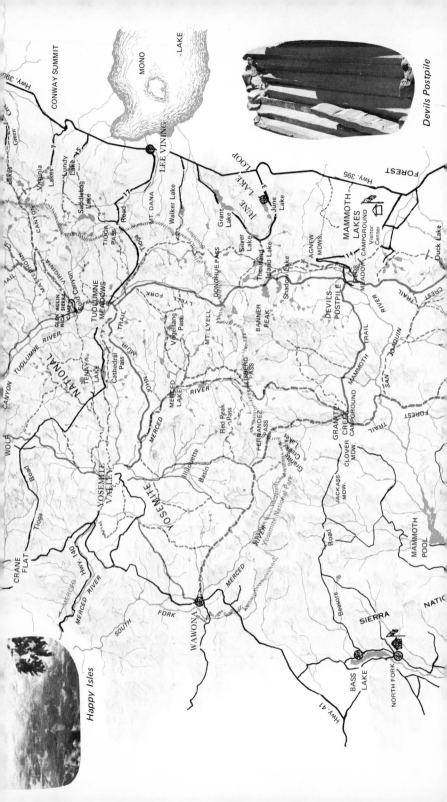

Devils Postpile

Happy Isles

John Muir Trail Country

Half Dome

Map labels:

BRIDGPORT

Toiyabe National Forest District Ranger Station

SONORA JUNCTION

FOREST

NATIONAL

Hwy. 395

Hwy. 108

Walker River

Robinson Creek

TWIN LAKES

Wilderne...

Little Walker River

Hoover

Buckeye Creek

BUCKEYE PASS

Leavitt Meadow

TOIYABE

PACIFIC CREST TRAIL

West Walker River

LEAVITT TRAIL

LEAVITT LAKE

BROWN BEAR PASS

DOROTHY LAKE PASS

Kerrick Canyon

PARK

CREST

BENSON LAKE

KENNEDY MEADOWS

SONORA PASS

Summit Creek

EMIGRANT LAKE

BOND PASS

TILDEN LAKE

JACK MAIN CANYON

WILMER LAKE

PACIFIC

DARDENELLE

FOREST

EMIGRANT BASIN WILDERNESS

HUCKLEBERRY LAKE

Kibbie Lake

LAKE ELEANOR

PATE VALLEY

GRAND

STANISLAUS RIVER

NATIONAL

CHERRY RESV.

CHERRY LAKE

HETCH HETCHY

MATHER

DONNELLS RESV.

STANISLAUS

PINECREST LAKE

PINECREST

Strawberry

STOCKTON

STANISLAUS

TUOLUMNE RIVER

Hwy. 120

MODESTO

Mountain Dogwood   Manzanita   Buttercup
Pride of the Mountains   Bigelow Sneezeweed Sierra Primrose
Geranium   Indian Paintbrush

Scarlet Mimulus
Yellow Throated Gilia
Owl's Clover

Red Heather
Scarlet Gilia
Yellow Columbine

Sneezweed
Bleeding Heart
Blazing Star

Tehipite Dome

Palisades Glacier

Mt. Whitney

Giant Sequoia

Leopard Lily
Labrador Tea
Pussy Paws

Monkey Flower
Sierra Star Tulip

Sky Pilot
Mimulus Lewisii

All photographs by Richard Burns, Asst. Chief Park Interpretater
Sequoia National Park

USE OF THIS GUIDE

Information in this guide represents a culmination of many years experience and journeys into the Sierra and almost as many months at the typewriter and drawing board. Effort has been made to present the maps in a style that gives a third dimension effect of the country from the air. Many of the elevation representations were drawn in the mountains combining topo readings with personal observation.

The Sierra Range has been divided into probable travel routes and destinations. Adjacent areas are shown in overlapping sequence. Quite a few are drawn to show where you are in relation to where you want to go on an ordinary mornings fishing trip - not in relation to Ursa Major. On such maps, directional arrows indicate north. If not shown, north is the top of the map.

Trail mileage data is presented in the Profile and is based upon the best information available.

Sequoia — Kings Canyon National Parks: Data based upon Park Engineers maps, trail signs, trail crew records, and personal travels.

Yosemite National Park: All trails were personally measured with a metered bicycle wheel and cross-checked with the Park Engineers maps.

National Forest and Wilderness Areas: Trail data checked with records of Patrol Rangers, Engineer's data, and general Forest Service maps.

All this information was balanced against data shown on USGS Topos to present a reasonable presentation of conditions and mileages between important places.

It is recommended that in addition to this guide book, back-country bound hikers planning to crosscountry, should secure a USGS topo quadrangle of the specific area they plan to visit, plus checking with the Ranger when securing your Wilderness Permit.

L E G E N D S and T R A I L S I G N S

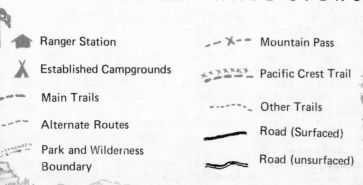

Ranger Station	Mountain Pass
Established Campgrounds	Pacific Crest Trail
Main Trails	Other Trails
Alternate Routes	Road (Surfaced)
Park and Wilderness Boundary	Road (unsurfaced)

"Duc"

Early Day "Blaze" **17**

Giant Forest

The Giant Forest entry into the southern Sierra lies in a setting that provides a wide range of experiences with the land, forest cover, and its wildlife. It is located on a rough bench at the extreme western edge of a huge mountain group that separates the Middle and Marble Forks of the Kaweah River and extends eastward to climax at Alta Peak.

Its several thousand acres affords optimum conditions for the development of such a varied forest. Here, deep soil that is well watered by heavy snow packs and an extensive southwestern exposure combine to produce an almost exhuberant flora. This forest's almost untouched survival can be credited to the more than five thousand foot difference in elevation between the Kaweah at Three Rivers (816') and Giant Forest (6,700'). Whenever you become discouraged with the long, hot, twisting road up the General's Highway from the Park entrance at Ash Mountain, remember it was this same climb when primitive road building met its match and forestalled loggers efforts to harvest this wondrous grove.

Most visitors arriving from almost sea level will experience some difficulty for a day or so at these elevations. It is highly recommended that hikers take it easy before attempting strenuous trips. Also, information available at the Lodgepole Visitor Center or at General Grove Museum as well as your own observations on some of the local trails will add much to your pleasure on more extended backcountry trips.

Several walks and trail trips are suggested for your wind and muscle before heading out for the Great Western Divide. Don't push it. The real enjoyment on walks and backpack trips happens along the way—not at any given destination, time, or place.

ACCOMMODATIONS AND SERVICES

Information Centers: National Park Service centers at Ash Mountain, Lodgepole, Grant Grove and Cedar Grove.

Stores: Giant Forest, Lodgepole, Stony Creek, Grant Grove and Cedar Grove Villages, and Wilsonia. Limited supplies available in winter at Giant Forest, Grant Grove Village and Wilsonia.

Mail Service: Post Offices in Lodgepole, Sequoia National Park, CA, 93262 (open all year) and Grant Grove, Kings Canyon National Park, CA, 93633 (summer only)

Service Stations: Lodgepole, Grant Grove and Cedar Grove.

Lodges: Giant Forest Lodge, Grant Grove Lodge, Cedar Grove Camp, and Bearpaw Meadow Camp.

Campgrounds: Potwisha, Buckeye, Lodgepole, Dorst, Stony Creek, Grant Grove, Cedar Grove, Atwell Mill, South Fork, Big Meadows, Hume Lake, Indian Basin, and Bearpaw Meadows.

Picnic Areas: Potwisha, Wolverton, Dorst, Big Stump Entrance, and Crescent Meadows.

GIANT FOREST AREA FOOT TRAILS
(one half to six mile walks)

Round Meadow: Includes forest area around meadow near Lodge and Village with side trips to Sunset Rock and Beetle Rock.

General Sherman/Congress Trail: (See map page 20) Loop trip 2.0 miles. Easy walk, first half paved. Trailhead south of parking lot.

Trial of the Sequoias: 5 - 6 miles. Is an extension of the Congress Trail to include Log Meadow, Tharps Log and west side of Crescent Meadow.

Huckleberry Meadow: 4 mile loop trip. Includes Indian mortars, Bear's Bathtub, Squatter's Cabin and Huckleberry Meadow.

Log Meadow: Starts at Crescent Meadow. Includes Log Meadow, Chimney Tree and area east of Crescent Meadow.

Moro Rock - Bear Hill Loop: (See map page 21) Parallels road 3.5 miles round trip. Many kinds of trees. Easy walk. Includes climb to top of Moro Rock and Hanging Rock. Exceptional views to west and south across Kaweah basin to Deer Ridge, Castle Rocks, and Great Western Divide.

Sugarpine Trail: Runs between Moro Rock and Crescent Meadow. 1.0 mile. Continuous pamorama of horizon from Moro Rock, mountains beyond Mineral King and Great Western Divide (follows almost level contour between road and edge of canyon).

LODGEPOLE AREA

Tokopah Valley: (4 miles, round trip) Follows along Marble Fork Kaweah River to Tokopah Valley (Indian term for "high mountain valley"). Exceptional high country type scenery. Ranger conducted walk every morning. Check at Visitor Center for information on this unusual, informative trip. Allow 3 - 5 hours round trip.

Lakes Trail: (Trailhead at Wolverton parking lot) about 9 miles round trip. Includes five small lakes, spectacular views. Some strenuous sections going out.

Alta Trail: (Trailhead at Wolverton Parking lot) 9 miles steady up hill all the way to the summit of Alta Peak (11,211'). Allow 7 - 9 hours round trip. Includes complete range of forest type from sequoias to above timberline. Tremendous 360 degree view. Even Mt. Whitney. Trail continues to lovely Moose Lake. Return could be by way of Hazelwood Picnic Area at Giant Forest Village.

CAR AND WALK TRIPS

Little Baldy: Trailhead located about 6 miles west of Lodgepole on General Highway. About two miles to top. Good views.

Muir Grove: Trailhead at Dorst Campground. 6 - 7 miles round trip. Exceptional grove of mature sequoias.

General Grant Grove: Several trails in area. Check at Visitor Center.

Cedar Grove/Zumwalt Meadow: Located on south Fork of Kings River. Half dozen special trail trips and some conducted motor tours, check at Visitor Center.

Crystal Cave: Located 9 miles west of Giant Forest Village. One half mile walk down to entrance. Trail well graded and surfaced. During summer Ranger conducted tours every hour. Exceptional cave experience. Take wraps.

Mineral King: Located across Kaweah Valley from Giant Forest. Road turn off at Hammond, Hwy. 198 just above Three Rivers. 25 miles of steep, winding road to Mineral King road end. Trails lead to lakes, sequoia groves and summit of Great Western Divide.

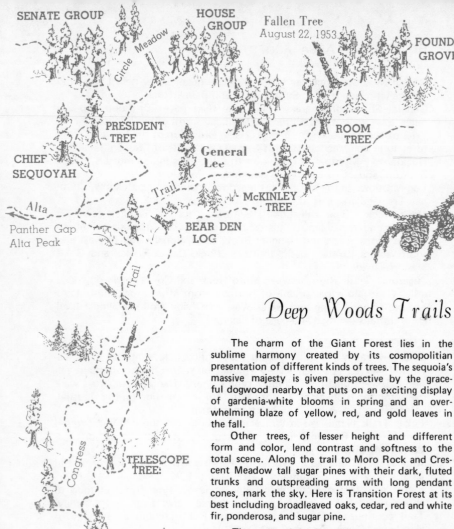

SENATE GROUP HOUSE GROUP Fallen Tree August 22, 1953 FOUNDED GROVE

Circle Meadow

PRESIDENT TREE General Lee ROOM TREE

CHIEF SEQUOYAH Trail McKINLEY TREE

Alta BEAR DEN LOG

Panther Gap
Alta Peak

Grove Trail

Congress

TELESCOPE TREE:

PARKING

GENERAL SHERMAN TREE

Deep Woods Trails

The charm of the Giant Forest lies in the sublime harmony created by its cosmopolitian presentation of different kinds of trees. The sequoia's massive majesty is given perspective by the graceful dogwood nearby that puts on an exciting display of gardenia-white blooms in spring and an overwhelming blaze of yellow, red, and gold leaves in the fall.

Other trees, of lesser height and different form and color, lend contrast and softness to the total scene. Along the trail to Moro Rock and Crescent Meadow tall sugar pines with their dark, fluted trunks and outspreading arms with long pendant cones, mark the sky. Here is Transition Forest at its best including broadleaved oaks, cedar, red and white fir, ponderosa, and sugar pine.

The route of the Deep Woods Trails include impressive associations with the Giant Sequoias that are found along the western slope of the Sierra between Sequoia and Yosemite - the southern and northern terminus points of the John Muir Trail Country.

The dense quiet of the deep woods is broken only by occasional treetop winds, the echoing notes of the Audubon warblers, or the gay chattering of the chickaree announcing the arrival of quests.

Age: Estimated at between 3,500 and 4,000 years old. The exact age of such trees can only be estimated in relation to other trees that have fallen or been cut and their annual rings counted.

Size: Height above mean base, 272.4 feet; Base circumference, 101.6 feet; Maximum base diameter, 36.5 feet; Mean base diameter, 32.2 feet; Weight of trunk (approx.) 625 tons; Total volume of trunk (approx.) 50,010 cubic feet; Height to first large branch, 130.0 feet; Diameter of first large branch, 6.8 feet; Length of first large limb, 140 feet. (This branch itself is larger than most trees east of the Mississippi River.)

IGH SIERRA TRAIL
Leading to Hamilton Lake
Kern River Country and
eventually to Mt. Whitney

Echo Point
Castle Rock View
Triple Tree

PARKER GROUP

Eagle View

Bobcat Point

Moro Vista
Hanging Rock

JEFFERSON TREE

Kaweah Vista

TUNNEL LOG

Sugar Pine Trail

BLACK CHAMBER

MATHER PLAQUE

Scarred Twin

AUTO LOG

Parking

CRESCENT MEADOW

Tharps Log

Log Meadow

Huckleberry Meadow

DOGWOOD

Forest Rim Trails

The setting of these two areas offer a balanced contrast of experiences. The Forest Rim Trails follow along the western and southern edge of the Giant Forest benchland. For some five miles, between the Village and Crescent Meadow area, it is a continuous, ever-changing panorama of typical southern Sierra landscape extending from the mile deep canyon before us to the 13,000' crest of the Great Western Divide to the east.

Interjected in pleasant relief are the nearby meadowed basins with their springs or meandering streams. With the change of the seasons, they present a succession of colors with their many flowers.

Coffee Shop

GIANT FOREST VILLAGE

Hazelwood Picnic area

Lodge

MORO ROCK A great dome formation similar to Tehipiti Dome found in the Kings Canyon and Half Dome in Yosemite. From its summit (Elev. 6,719'), can be had a magnificent view of the great river basins and low ridges to the west that are contrasted with the precipitous canyon walls to the east that terminate in the craggy crest of the Great Western Divide. This is often mistaken for the Sierra crest and many think they see Mt. Whitney there. It is probably Sawtooth Peak they see as Mt. Whitney lies out of sight farther to the east. The great Kern River basin lies between the Great Western Divide and the main Sierra crest.

CRESCENT MEADOW John Muir once referred to this as the most beautiful of Sierra meadows. In size, form, and the life that surrounds it the meadow presents a scene of rare beauty. The area is noted for its many wildflowers in spring and is an excellent place to observe many kinds of birds. The tiny stream at the lower end contains a few small Eastern brook trout that are a delight to the children to watch. (Note: Positively NO fishing is permitted here!)

The High Sierra Trail leading to Hamilton Lake, the Kern River Country, and eventually to Mt. Whitney, has its beginning here near the parking lot. Other trails lead to Tharps Log, the Chimney Tree, Kaweah Vista, and Giant Forest Village. From Eagle View nearby (1.0) there is an expansive view that truly emphasizes the Sequoia-Kings Canyon country as "a land of giant trees, deep canyons, and high mountains."

Great Western Divide

Wayne Alcorn, NPS, Sequoia

An unusual, well developed trail up the 600' ascent includes steps and handrails. At the top of the dome a 360 degree view gives the grand sweep of the western Sierra. An orientation plaque at the summit indicates salient points on the horizon.

Moro Rock   Wayne Alcorn, NPS

Crescent Meadow — Wayne Alcorn, NPS

HIGH SIERRA TRAIL

EAGLE VIEW PT.	1	KAWEAH GAP	20
PANTHER CREEK	3	NINE LAKES BASIN	21
BUCK CANYON	10	BIG ARROYO	23
BEARPAW MDW.	11½	LITTLE FIVE L.	27
RIVER VALLEY	13	CHAGOOPA PLATEAU	28
LONE PINE CREEK	13	MORAINE LAKE	30
ELIZABETH PASS	16	KERN CANYON	40
HAMILTON LAKE	16	KERN HOT SPRINGS	42
DEADMAN CANYON	19	JUNCTION MDW.	50
REDWOOD MEADOW	19	CRABTREE MDW.	62
MINERAL KING	30	MT. WHITNEY	70
KINGS CANYON	37	LONE PINE (HWY)	92

CRESCENT MEADOW TRAILHEAD TO THE HIGH SIERRA

The High Sierra Trail, one of the finest in the west, combines a maximum of scenic variety with a minimum of effort. Beginning at Crescent Meadow (6,700') it follows along the high shoulder of the canyon almost a mile above the Kaweah River. West of the Kaweah Gap most of the trail is between 8,000' to 10,000'. After crossing the Great Western Divide at Kaweah Gap (10,700'), it drops down into the Big Arroyo, follows along the shoulders of the Kaweah Peaks to the Moraine Lake — Chagoopa Plateau area (9,000' - 9,500'). Descending the abrupt western wall of the Kern Canyon, it crosses the Kern River (6,600'), then follows the almost level floor for nearly ten miles. It then makes a 2,500' climb in some five miles to join the John Muir Trail at Wallace Creek.

23

High Sierra Trail

For the first twelve miles out of Crescent Meadow, this route presents a continuous panorama of the Kaweah Basin and the crest of the Great Western Divide. After leaving Bearpaw Meadow it climbs to the Hamilton Lakes. Above the Lakes the canyon becomes much narrower. Two miles east, tunnels have been blasted out of the solid rock wall where steep cliffs above the long drop-off into the river below provide a thrilling contrast to the first days saunter between Crescent Meadow and Hamilton Lakes.

One of the easiest passes in the Sierra is over the Kaweah Gap. From its rounded summit the views westward toward the Kaweah Basin extend to the San Joaquin Valley. To the east we look down into the headwaters of the Kern. Across the Big Arroyo stands the Kaweah Ridge with the Red, Black, and Kaweah peaks cresting over 13,000'.

Just below the Kaweah Gap, an excellent crosscountry alternate route to the upper Kern can be made by bearing north through the Nine Lakes Basin, over an easy crossing of the Kaweah Ridge, south of the Triple Divide Peak. The trail then follows the Kern-Kaweah River down to join the Colby Pass Trail just above Gallats Lake, passes Rockslide Lake, then down to meet the High Sierra Trail at Junction Meadow. Experienced hikers will enjoy the climbs along the Kaweah highlands and the less frequently visited Kaweah Basin.

Descending along the stream between Eagle Scout Peak and the Kaweah peaks, the High Sierra Trail at first follows along, then gradually climbs to the high, north shoulder of the Big Arroyo to the Chagoopa Plateau. The extensive flower-strewn meadow country of this plateau and Sky Parlor Meadow present continuous temptations in photography as the sky becomes filled with bellowing white clouds heralding the arrival of a possible afternoon shower. The alternate trail including Moraine Lake, a photography classic among Sierra travelers, follows close to the crest of the Big Arroyo and rejoins the High Sierra Trail at Sky Parlor Meadow.

GIANT FOREST – GREAT WESTERN DIVIDE 21.5
(via High Sierra Trail to Kaweah Gap)

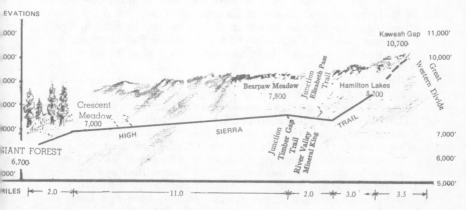

Kaweah Gap — Hamilton Lake

NPS, Sequoia

Other Entries from the West:

MINERAL KING: One route crosses the Great Western Divide at Sawtooth or Franklin passes, then follows down the Big Arroyo to join the Kern near Funston Meadow. (35 - 50 miles)

A second trip crosses at Timber Gap, follows down Cliff Creek to Redwood Meadow Grove of giant sequoias, then up the Kaweah River Valley to Bearpaw Meadows. A side trip can be made to Pinto Lake, then over the Black Rock Pass to the Little Five Lakes and Big Five Lakes, going north to meet the High Sierra Trail at the Big Arroyo below Kaweah Gap.

LODGEPOLE/HORSE CORRAL: An unusually good route in early season. Sugarloaf Country is a warm, open forest country. Cloud Canyon, Colby Pass and the Kern-Kaweah provides A-plus scenery.

CEDAR GROVE/COPPER CREEK: This route includes Sphinx Creek, Colby Pass as an alternate to the Horse Corral route above, or via the more traveled Bubbs Creek and Forester Pass Country.

Another interesting, less traveled trip is by way of Sphinx Creek. Crossing the crest at Avalanche Pass, then fording Roaring River near the Ranger Station, it ascends Deadman Canyon to Elizabeth Pass. The trail then descends in switchbacks, crossing Lone Pine Creek to meet the High Sierra Trail between Bearpaw Meadow and Hamilton

Lakes.

The Kern River Basin

The views from the shoulder of the tremendous Kern River Canyon extends north to Forester Pass country on the Kings-Kern Divide, south along the Plateau country, and east across the mountain-strewn bench of its climax along the Whitney-Muir Crest. From here, for nearly five miles, the trail switchbacks down the canyon wall to cross the Kern River at Upper Funston Meadow.

The river maintains an almost true north-south course more than 70 miles down this glacial-worn trough. Its floor is quite level, gravelly, and dry. Except in early season, this is a warm, dry trail. Vegetation is sparse, with little grass, sagebrush is common, semi-desert in spots - complete with lizards and snakes. Trees are typical of 5,000' - 6,000' elevations.

The northern limit of the 10,000' Kern Plateau lies between the crescent shaped mountains to the east and the deep, Kern Canyon to the west. Multi-lake basins are found along the Sierra crest at the headwaters of Rock, Whitney, Wallace, and Tyndall creeks. All invite extended fishing and scenic ventures.

iamond Mesa, south of Forester Pass

W. H. Paine

28

The Kern River country has long been famous for its plunging waters and fighting rainbow trout. But remember, the big ones didn't get that way from being careless in their feeding habits. However, S-P-L (skill, patience, luck) will provide a good meal for supper most anywhere in this country.

Many a skinny dip has been made in the Kern Hot Springs located near the river about 2.5 miles above Upper Funston crossing. Just before the Hot Springs, across the river, the Chagoopa Creek comes tumbling down from its high plateau origins in a succession of cascades and small falls ending in a total drop of 1,600' into the Kern Canyon.

HAMILTON LAKES — UPPER FUNSTON MEADOW 19.0
(via Kaweah Gap, Big Arroyo, Moraine Lake)

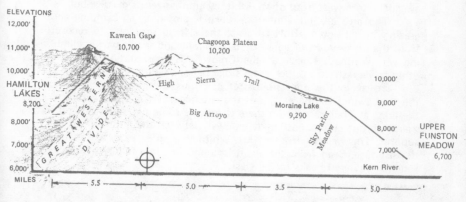

UPPER FUNSTON MEADOW — MT. WHITNEY 26.5
(via Wallace Creek, Crabtree Meadow)

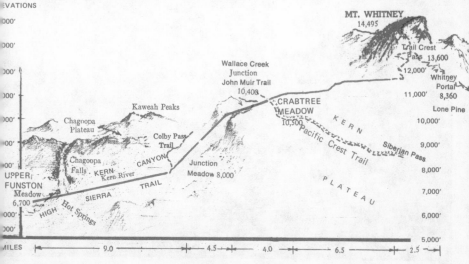

29

The High Sierra Trail follows along the east side of the river nearly ten miles to Junction Meadow. There the Kern-Kaweah River and Wallace Creek add their waters to the growing Kern. Trails lead to the Kern—Kaweah River to Colby Pass; up the Kern to Milestone and Lake South America basins; then east up Wallace Creek to junction with the John Muir Trail, which is almost halfway between Foresters Pass and the summit of Mt. Whitney.

At Whitney Creek is the meeting place for the John Muir Trail extending from Whitney Portal to Yosemite Valley; the Pacific Crest Trail route running from the Mexican to the Canadian borders; and trails leading to the Cottonwood Lakes and the Golden Trout country.

The John Muir Trail between Wallace Creek and Mt. Whitney includes a most appropriate approach for your ascent to the mountain. Contrasted to the rough, foxtail pine forested plateau and the extensive meadows at Crabtree Meadows, the route up Whitney Creek, past Timberline and several smaller lakes is most delightful. The great avalanche torn west front of Mt. Whitney emphasizes its massive bulk.

The area around Timberline Lake is closed to all camping and grazing in a belated effort to assist these fragil meadows to recover from the many years of abuse by large hiking and saddle parties climbing Mt. Whitney. Check at the Crabtree Ranger Station regarding other travel restrictions such as no stock beyond Guitar Lake, etc.

To avoid the impassible stretches, plus continuous rock slides, the trail swings to the east, past the Hitchcock Lakes, then climbs to the crest at Trail Pass. From there it follows some two miles along the sharp, abrupt crest - passing "windows" between the pinnacles to the summit. The western front of Mt. Whitney is an extreme contrast to its east face. Seen from the air, it becomes lost in a family of similar round-shouldered peaks to the west.

Mt. Whitney From the West   Bill Jones, NPS, Sequoia

W

Southern Sierra Crest — Mt. Whitney (W)

Rocky Rockwell, USFS

31

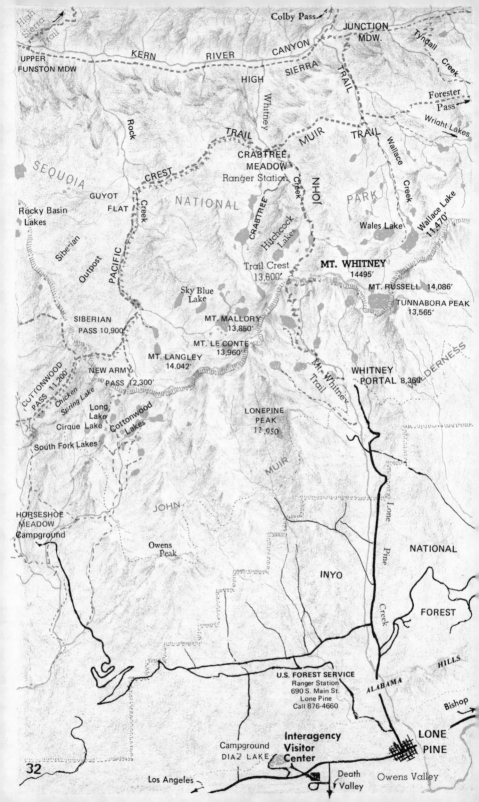

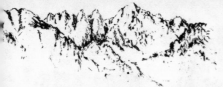

Mt. Whitney Trail

The Mt. Whitney Trail, built and maintained by the U.S. Forest Service is much traveled and very spectacular. Its upper portion is through open, barren country with little vegetation and no water the last several miles. DANGER: Attempt no shortcuts! To do so is to invite disaster to yourself, those along the trail below you, and those who may have to help you if you get into trouble.

Most anyone in reasonably good physical condition can make the trip in two days without difficulty. In recent years as many as 10,000 people have climbed Mt. Whitney, with a record of some 600 on a Labor Day weekend. Such numbers made it necessary to establish a quota system on overnight trips, limiting it to 75 per day.

A one-day trip is out of the question for most people with the arduous climb from 8,000' at Whitney Portal up to 14,495' at the top. Every summer nearly all who try a one-day trip fail after an exhausting, disappointing experience. Plan ahead! Get your Wilderness Permit at Lone Pine for an overnight trip. Leave your car at Whitney Portal and get up as far as Trail Camp for your overnight bivouac; then, leaving early next morning, you will have a real mountain adventure with daylight breaking over the eastern basin ranges to light your way.

To those who just insist on climbing mountains the hard way, the east face presents a challenge to the best of them. It is to be strictly avoided by the inexperienced mountain climber. This route follows up the east fork of Lone Pine Creek to the base of the mountain. From there several ways confront the climber. The Mountaineers Route was first used by John Muir on October 21, 1873. This is a Class 2 climb. Some half dozen other routes requiring special equipment range between Class 4 and Class 6. Some are unsound and several climbers have been killed in their attempts. Do not climb this mountain until you have carefully checked your route with those issuing permits.

CRABTREE MEADOW — LONE PINE 23.5
(via Trail Crest Pass, Whitney Portal)

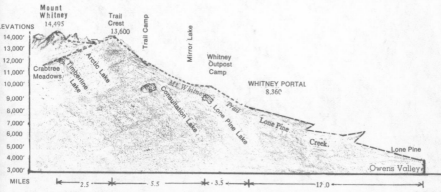

Summit with Smithsonian Hut   Eugene Ros

34   Whitney Pinnacles   Rocky Rockwell, USFS

WHAT IS IT LIKE ON TOP?

It's simply tremendous! To the north and west the view is a continuous landscape of barren rock pushed up from deep in the earth in the ancient past and now shaped into deep river valleys, glacial cirques, and ragged ranges which extend off into the blue mists of the distant horizon.

To the east is the sweep of the Owens River basin lying more than 10,000' below. At night can be seen the lights of Lone Pine. Beyond there lies the desert basins of the Mojave and Death Valley country, much of which lies far below sea level. Nearby, along the Muir Crest, can be seen seven of the eleven peaks of the Sierra whose summits exceed 14,000'

The summit itself is about one and a half acres in area and is quite flat. It is abruptly precipitous several thousand feet on the east face but to the west it slopes off into a steeply rounded shoulder that is furrowed by deep gullies formed by avalanches of snow and rocks. The almost table-like summit is littered with huge granite boulders and slabs which have a distinct type of weathering called nivation — the result of prolonged action by frost. Little, if any, effect of erosion by water can be seen because nearly all precipitation at this elevation falls in the form of snow rather than rain. The heavier winter snows have little effect on the rock as the surface is exposed to stiff prevailing winds which keep it swept clear of deep drifts. What snow remains disappears mostly through evaporation rather than by melting and stream-type runoff.

Near the eastern lip of the summit is a small, two-room stone building. It was built by the Smithsonian Institute years ago as a shelter for scientists who stayed up there making observations.

East Front — Climbers Route   Rocky Rockwell, USFS

Mineral King is a center to a fascinating region. It is an undeveloped, quiet, secluded Valley of sup-alpine character surrounded by towering crests of the Great Western Divide. Trips westward to Hockett Meadows include the Atwell, Garfield and Eden sequoia groves, Clough Cave, and many high basin lakes to satisfy the angler. To the south, White Chief, Eagle and Mosquito lakes provide unusual scenic grandeur. The upper Little Kern Country is reached just beyond Farewell Gap.

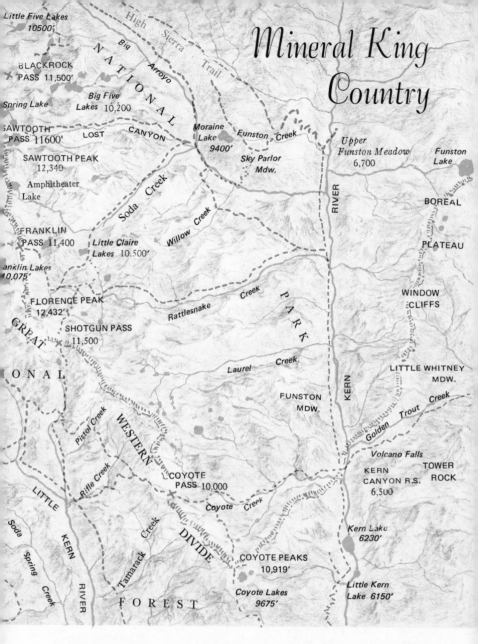

Mineral King Country

Little Five Lakes
10500'

BLACKROCK
PASS 11,500'

Spring Lake

Big Five
Lakes 10,200

SAWTOOTH
PASS 11600'

LOST CANYON

Moraine
Lake
9400'

Funston Creek

Upper
Funston Meadow
6,700

Funston
Lake

SAWTOOTH PEAK
12,340

Sky Parlor
Mdw.

BOREAL

Amphitheater
Lake

Soda Creek

PLATEAU

FRANKLIN
PASS 11,400

Willow Creek

Little Claire
Lakes 10.500'

WINDOW
CLIFFS

anklin Lakes
10,075'

FLORENCE PEAK
12,432'

Rattlesnake Creek

PARK

LITTLE WHITNEY
MDW.

GREAT

SHOTGUN PASS
11,500

Laurel Creek

KERN

FUNSTON
MDW.

Golden Trout Creek

ONAL

Pistol Creek

WESTERN

Volcano Falls

KERN
CANYON R.S.
6,500

TOWER
ROCK

LITTLE

Rifle Creek

COYOTE
PASS 10,000

Coyote Creek

Kern Lake
6230'

Soda

Spring Creek

KERN RIVER

Tamarack Creek

DIVIDE

COYOTE PEAKS
10,919'

Coyote Lakes
9675'

Little Kern
Lake 6150'

FOREST

Trails east lead down Rattlesnake Creek or Lost Canyon to junction with the famous Kern River Canyon. Also, to the new Golden Trout Wilderness Area or up the Kern to meet the High Sierra Trail.

It is an ideal family camping country. Services include a small store with limited supplies and saddle stock. Parking space for backcountry hikers is very limited.

EXPLORING THE
Great Western Divide
FROM MINERAL KING

Mineral King is an ideal trailhead for circling the Great Western Divide or going alternate routes to the upper Kern country. Any trip that covers Colby Pass, down Cloud Canyon, and up over Elizabeth Pass will be long remembered.

Numerous lakes, especially Amphitheater or Columbine, or such groups as the beautiful Big or Little Five lakes and the Nine Lakes Basin along the east side of the Divide provide excellent fishing. Entry to this area is via the Black Rock, Sawtooth, or Franklin passes.

The Kern River Country

John Muir Trail travelers pausing at the crest of the Kings-Kern Divide at Forester Pass, have spread below them the far reaching panorama of the famous Kern River Country. Here the Sierra crest, almost as if it held more than it could accommodate in one range, splits into two commanding arms.

To the east stands a grand array of peaks well above 13,000' surrounding Mt. Whitney so close it appears more as an equal member of a family group rather than an individual spectacle of nature.

To the west and south runs the Great Western Divide separating the waters of the Kern and Kaweah Rivers with a long chain of peaks and crests ranging between 12,000' to 13,000'. It extends southward well beyond the Mineral King basin and divides the waters of the main Kern River canyon from its western tributary — the Little Kern.

The South Fork of the Kern, largest of the Kern tributaries, rises in the famous Golden Trout Country near Siberian Pass. Its southward course on the Kern Plateau from Big Whitney Meadow parallels the Sierra crest for some 40 miles to Rockhouse Basin. Below there it begins its drop in a succession of twisting torrents and cascades for ten miles to the South Fork Valley where it turns on its westward course for confluence with the main Kern at Isabella Lake.

It is a region varied in geographic structure and the wildlife it supports from sage, chaparral, and oak lowlands to its long eastern lodgepole and foxtail pine slopes.

From Kernville, trails lead north to the Plateau region to Sequoia National Park also east to the new permanent Pacific Crest Trail.

Several trailheads lead to the Little Kern basin out of Johnsondale, Camp Nelson, Camp Wishon and Balch Park. Entry to Sequoia National Park via Summit Lake and Hockett Meadows can also be made via trails from here. An unusual trip could include several routes between Mineral King and Burnt Corral Meadows. This would provide camping at Hockett Lakes, a choice of several routes over the Great Western Divide, and the upper Kern Canyon to Golden Trout Creek.

Entry from the north can be made via Three Rivers. From there a road climbs steeply 12 miles to Clough Cave Ranger Station to beautiful seldom visited country. Here lies the headwaters of the South Fork of the Kaweah. Its charm includes the Garfield Groves, broad plateau meadows, and numerous lakes.

DOMELAND WILDERNESS

The unusual type, and number of granite domes in this area of the Kern Plateau has given it its name and status as a Wilderness Area. Its elevation range from 3000' to some 9000' plus its exposure on the southern slope-down of the Sierra block gives it a semi-arid, desert-type climate that supports a limited variety of vegetation. Mixed conifers and pinons make up most of the larger trees on the higher slopes while sage and desert flora extends into the lower elevations.

As a whole, the area is extremely rugged — much of it considered inaccessible along the South Fork of the Kern that flows through it. Here it is appropriately called *The Roughs*.

Wilderness Permits and the latest information are available at Cannell Meadows District Ranger Office. The roads are mostly dirt, gravel with some blacktop. Some definitely are not suitable for passenger cars so be sure to check before entering this wilderness area. No ORV's are permitted in this region.

Pacific Crest Trail

The new route of the Pacific Crest Trail now crosses the Sequoia National Park boundary between the New Army Pass and Siberian Pass. It swings eastward along the rim of the Cottonwood Creek Basin to Cottonwood Pass and Mulkey Pass, then down along the eastern edge of the Kern Plateau, and the South Fork of the Kern River. There are seven small holding corrals for wrangler's stock located in various places along the route. These are marked on the map.

EASTERN ENTRY POINTS: (1) Horseshoe Meadows, out of Lone Pine. (2) Sage Flat Road, five miles south of Olancha. A dry, hot trail to Olancha Pass in mid-summer. (3) Haiwee Creek Road, north of Little Lake. (4) Nine-Mile Canyon Road at Pearsonville which goes to Chimney Creek Campground, Kennedy Meadows, and Osa Meadows.

Golden Trout Wilderness

The magnificent Kern and its tributaries have long been recognized for its excellent fishing and hunting. Its high streams and lakes are the home of the unique Golden Trout. They are found in the Little Kern, South Fork of the Kern River, and Cottonwood Lakes areas. The Kern River rainbows are also legion.

The newly created Golden Trout Wilderness (306,000 acres) includes the Little Kern River Basin, the northern Kern Plateau, and the southern part of Inyo National Forest adjacent to the John Muir Wilderness. It includes high country above timberline as well as extensive areas forested with oaks, firs and pines.

Its early spring, and numerous entry points (see map and profile) will insure good fishing, hunting, and camping experiences in a region that will be always preserved from motor travel and commercial activity. Many long established trails provide access to this area.

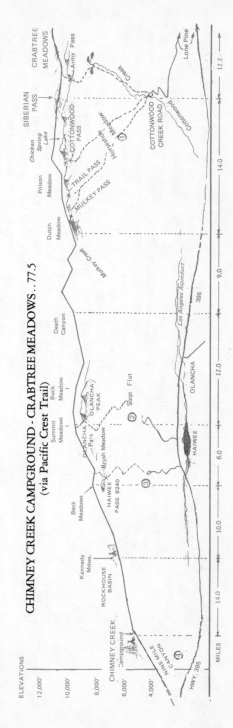

CHIMNEY CREEK CAMPGROUND - CRABTREE MEADOWS .. 77.5
(via Pacific Crest Trail)

Pacific Crest Trail

Pathfinders and trail builders have always had a profound influence on the course of our American progress and heritage. Our Daniel Boones and Jedediah Smiths expand the unknown valleys and mountain passes leading to them until exploration became idealized as a way of life. A way we will always feel when we seek mountains as an escape from urbanism.

With the final determination of trans-continental routes, the dreamers needed new horizons to explore in wilderness trails. For several decades proposals have evolved from individuals, groups, and now governmental agencies urging the creation of a national program of trails. To date approval has been given in planning and fiscal forms to complete a Pacific Crest National Scenic Trail that would provide a continuous route some 2,500 miles long between Mexico and Canada.

The planned route traverses lands and climates from the aird desert flats near Tecate east of San Diego to the snow covered peaks at the Canadian boundary of North Cascades National Park. To get such a monumental project into action required the combined efforts of such government agencies as the Forest Service, Bureau of Land Management and the National Park Service, as well as dozens of state, and local political units in Washington, Oregon and California.

Capitalizing upon existance of the' Oregon Skyline Trail, Cascade Crest Trail (Washington), and the John Muir Trail in the California Sierra, the minimum ingredients of the proposed trail were determined. Between these well developed routes some trails have been designated as temporary routes. In many places no trails actually exist and maps only show dotted lines labeled "proposed route". These vary from time to time on new maps.

Aside from the Muir Trail and a few sections of old trails originally built by army and pioneer foresters much needs to be done before it can be actually considered a Pacific Crest Trail suitable for continuous travel from Mexico to Canada.

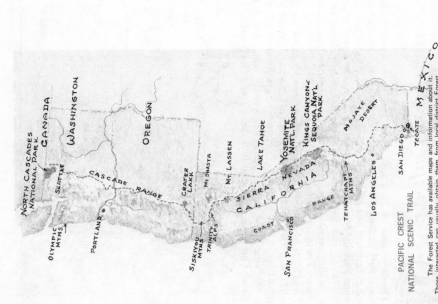

PACIFIC CREST
NATIONAL SCENIC TRAIL

The Forest Service has available maps and information about it.
Those interested can usually obtain them from local district. Forest
Service Offices, or write direct to the U.S. Forest Service; Division of

42

Kern Plateau Trail

The old temporary route of the Pacific Crest Trail from Kernville to the Siberian Pass is referred to in this guide as the Kern Plateau Trail. It is a medium level, north-south way with a number of entry points from both west and east sides.

In the past this trail has been used for recreational and commercial activities. It has not been satisfactory as a high country experience for backpackers due to the use by cattlemen, lumber trucks, and wheeled vehicles. Trails are well built and marked and its accessibility is enhanced by several roads as shown on the map page 40.

From Kernville, trails and roads lead to the Plateau country and east to the Pacific Crest Trail. From Osa Meadows (just south of Casa Vieja) it is eight miles across to the PCT at Summit Meadows near Olancha Pass. As an eastern entry to this region, the Nine-Mile Canyon Road extends as far up as Osa Meadows. These trails and roads tie into routes covering the Kern River and Plateau country opening an extensive region of little traveled routes through excellent camping country of forests and fishing.

KERNVILLE — CRABTREE MEADOW (Jctn. Muir Trail) 75.5

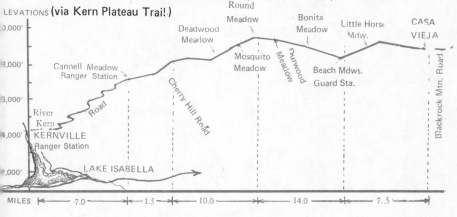

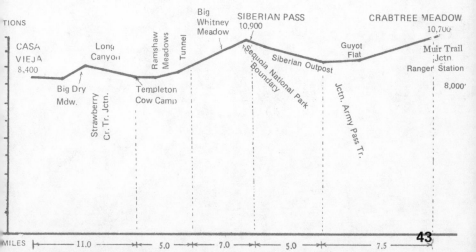

Kings - Kern Divide

Forester Pass, highest of the Muir Trail crossings at the crest of the Kings-Kern Divide, is an unusual skyline experience. The trail is well maintained, secure passages, giving breathtaking panorama views — to the north the grand peaks of the headwaters of the Kings River, to the south across and down the tremendous basin of the Kern.

Between Mt. Whitney and Woods Creek the Muir Trail route includes a region that has almost an excess of "High Sierra" rugged grandeur. The east access out of Cedar Grove and Onion Valley, and the inevitable heavy traffic up Bubbs Creek and over Kearsarge Pass makes it necessary to restrict the number who may secure permits each day. This allows only an overnight stop in some places and the request of non-wood cooking practices.

WALLACE CREEK — WOODS CREEK . . . 30.0
(via Forester Pass, Glen Pass, Rae Lakes)

Forester Pass

Suggested Side Trips off Main Trail
(Miles are approx. one-way)

1. Wales and Wright Lakes — 5
2. Wright Lakes — 4
3. Kern-Kaweah Basin — 5
4. Lake South America — 2
5. Milestone Basin — 6
6. Center Basin — 4

Cedar Grove, Kings Canyon National Park   NPS

CEDAR GROVE

Trailhead to the Upper Kings River Country

Here, from more than a thousand square miles of granite walled canyons, flow the waters from the northern slopes of the Great Western and Kings-Kern divides and from as far north as the headwaters of the South Fork of the Kings at Mather Pass.

In this deep valley early Indians made their homes in summer and established trade routes through the Bubbs Creek and Woods Creek canyons to exchange acorns for obsidian with the people from over the mountain in the Owens Valley.

Today's trails follow much the same ancient routes: the canyons to the right following along Bubbs Creek and over Kearsarge Pass. The left fork swinging almost due north through lovely Paradise Valley before turning east to Sierra crossings between Baxter and Taboose passes.

The valleys secluded position has discouraged development. Few commercial facilities exist, as basically it is an area inviting family camping and serves appropriately as a base for a number of trailheads into the rugged mountains of the mighty Kings.

Most of these trips can be planned to cross or include portions of the John Muir Trail. North-south trips west of the Muir Trail are, on the whole, at lower, warmer elevations where the forest cover assures top camping conditions. Wood, water, fishing and feed for stock are plentiful. If you want a real "back country experience", go into the back country, where the visitor count is low and camping is a joy.

Kings River Country

From Cedar Grove or Copper Creek trailheads, the divide offers challenging, remote, and rewarding trips via Kennedy or Granite passes to Simpson Meadows. Highly recommended are side trips to State or Horseshoe lakes, or a tour to the Goat Crest — Cirque Crest lakes. Return to Cedar Grove via Palisade Creek, Mather Pass and Pinchot Pass and Paradise Valley.

Caution: This is rugged country. Take it easy. If you are not an experienced backpacker when you start, you will be by the time you get back. Use extra care on any cross country ventures up there in Paradise and take NO shortcuts. As one old packer remarked, "It's sure great up there, but ain't no place to be wandering around in the dark!"

From Simpson Meadows on the Middle Fork there are several choices: Join up with the John Muir Trail at Grouse Meadows and, to make a loop trip, return to Cedar Grove via Rae Lakes, and either Woods or Bubbs creeks. Or turn west down the Kings to Tehipite Valley. From there ascend the canyon wall to Tehipite Dome to Crown Valley and explore the magnificent fishing and scenic country that is included in the Sierra Forest Trails of the John Muir Wilderness between Blackcap Basin and Hell-for-Sure Pass. For more information check maps beginning page 96.

CEDAR GROVE — SIMPSON MEADOW 31.5
(via Kennedy Pass, Dougherty Creek)

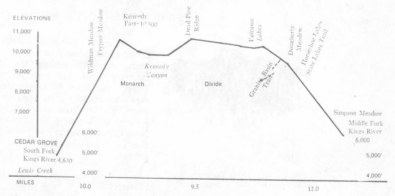

CEDAR GROVE — SOUTH LAKE (Parchers) 48.0
(via Granite Basin, Simpson Meadow, Bishop Pass)

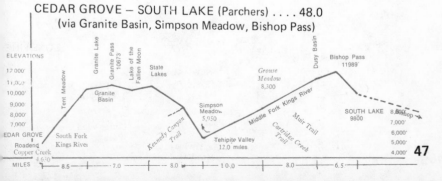

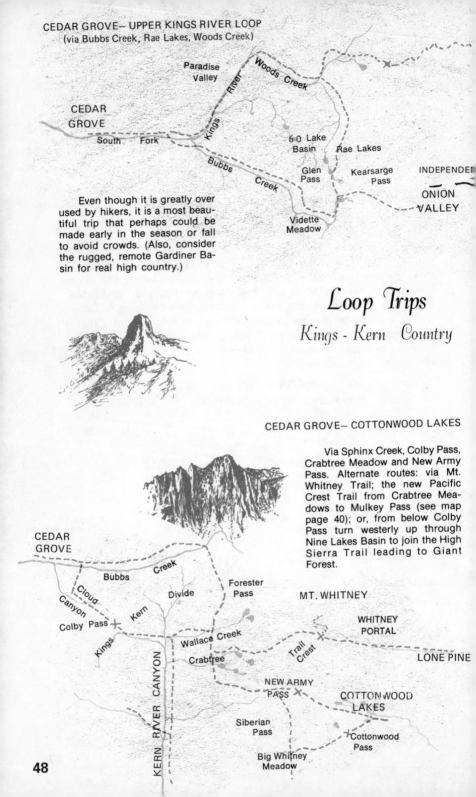

CEDAR GROVE— UPPER KINGS RIVER LOOP
(via Bubbs Creek, Rae Lakes, Woods Creek)

Paradise Valley

Woods Creek

CEDAR GROVE

South Fork

Kings River

Bubbs Creek

6 0 Lake Basin

Rae Lakes

Glen Pass

Kearsarge Pass

Vidette Meadow

INDEPENDE

ONION VALLEY

Even though it is greatly over used by hikers, it is a most beautiful trip that perhaps could be made early in the season or fall to avoid crowds. (Also, consider the rugged, remote Gardiner Basin for real high country.)

Loop Trips
Kings - Kern Country

CEDAR GROVE— COTTONWOOD LAKES

Via Sphinx Creek, Colby Pass, Crabtree Meadow and New Army Pass. Alternate routes: via Mt. Whitney Trail; the new Pacific Crest Trail from Crabtree Meadows to Mulkey Pass (see map page 40); or, from below Colby Pass turn westerly up through Nine Lakes Basin to join the High Sierra Trail leading to Giant Forest.

CEDAR GROVE

Bubbs Creek

Cloud Canyon

Colby Pass

Kern

Kings

Divide

Forester Pass

MT. WHITNEY

WHITNEY PORTAL

Wallace Creek

Crabtree

Trail Crest

LONE PINE

KERN RIVER CANYON

NEW ARMY PASS

COTTONWOOD LAKES

Siberian Pass

Cottonwood Pass

Big Whitney Meadow

Headwaters of Bubbs Creek

Bill Jones, NPS

CEDAR GROVE – ONION VALLEY 36.5
(via Paradise Valley, Rae Lakes, Kearsarge Pass)

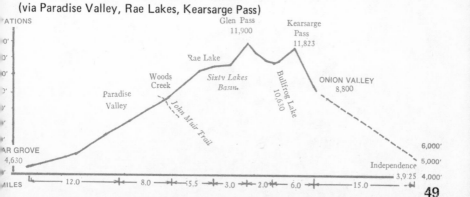

ELEVATIONS

Glen Pass
11,900

Kearsarge
Pass
11,823

Rae Lake

Woods
Creek

Sixty Lakes
Basin

ONION VALLEY
8,800

Paradise
Valley

John Muir Trail

Bullfrog Lake
10,650

6,000'

CEDAR GROVE
4,630

Independence

5,000'

4,000'

MILES — 12.0 — 8.0 — 5.5 — 3.0 — 2.0 — 6.0 — 15.0 — 3.9 25

49

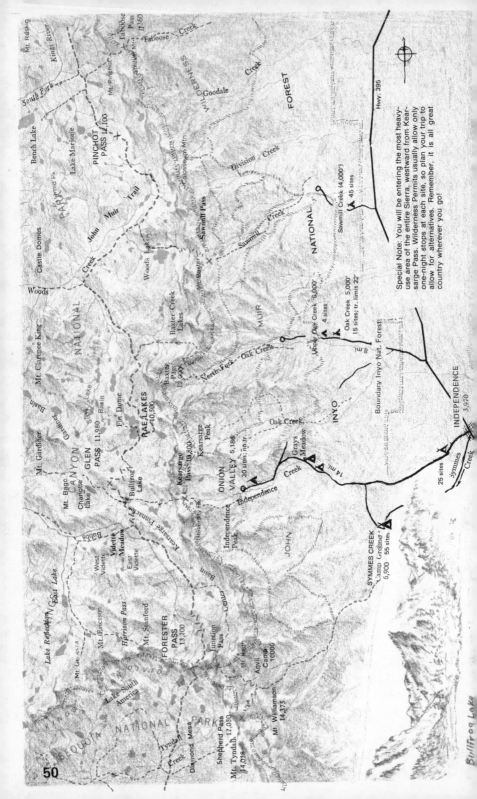

Special Note: You will be entering the most heavy-use area of the entire Sierra, westward from Kearsarge Pass. Wilderness Permits usually allow only one-night stops at each site, so plan your trip to allow for alternatives. Remember, it is all great country wherever you go!

Sawmill Creek (4,000') 45 sites

Upper Oak Creek 5,000' 4 sites

Oak Creek 5,000' 15 sites; tr. limit 22'

Boundary Inyo Nat. Forest

INDEPENDENCE 3,970

Hwy. 395

INYO

NATIONAL

FOREST

WILDERNESS

PINCHOT PASS 12,100

John Muir Trail

Sawmill Pass

Mt. Ruskin

Kings River

South Fork

Fatoose Creek

Taboose Pass 11,360

Creek

Goodale Creek

Division Creek

Mt. Pinchot

Lake Marjorie

Bench Lake

Castle Domes

Woods

Woods Creek

Woods Lakes

Colosseum Mtn.

Mt. Baxter

Baxter Creek Lakes

Baxter Pass 13,000'

North Fork — Oak Creek

Oak Creek

KINGS CANYON NATIONAL PARK

Mt. Clarence King

Mt. Gardiner

Gardiner Basin

Mt. Bago

Charlotte Lake

Fin Dome

Sixty Lake Basin

RAE LAKES 10,560

GLEN PASS 11,980

Kearsarge Lakes

Kearsarge Pass 10,800

Kearsarge Peak

Bullfrog Lake

Bubbs Creek

Vidette Meadow

West Vidette

East Vidette

Kearsarge Pinnacles

University Pk.

Center Basin

Independence Peak

ONION VALLEY 5,186 30 sites; no tr.

Independence

Grays Meadow

Independence Creek

14 mi.

25 sites

Symmes Creek

SYMMES CREEK Camp Ground 6,900 55 sites.

Lake Reflection

East Lake

Mt. Genevra

Mt. Ericsson

Mt. Stanford

Harrison Pass

Junction Pass

FORESTER PASS 13,200

Lake South America

GREAT WESTERN DIVIDE

Anvil Camp 10000

Mt. Keith

Mt. Williamson 14,375

JOHN MUIR WILDERNESS

Center Creek

SEQUOIA NATIONAL PARK

Tyndall Creek

Diamond Mesa

Shepherd Pass 12,050

Mt. Tyndall 14,018

Bullfrog Lake

50

Onion Valley-Kearsarge Pass

The Onion Valley/Kearsarge Pass route is the easiest and most used of the southern Sierra crossings leading to the upper Kings and Kern basins. Shepherd and Baxter passes are not too well developed or maintained. Both are long, arduous routes where special travel regulations apply. The Junction Pass Trail, no longer maintained, was part of the Muir Trail route before Forester Pass was opened.

The California Bighorn Sheep Zoological Area includes the high, eastern Sierra between Tunnabora Peak near Mt. Whitney to Mt. Perkins north of Sawmill Pass. Entry to the entire region is by limited passage through narrow corridors accommodating the trails.

Kearsarge Pass

Rocky Rockwell, USFS

52

Here in the space of a few days, the traveler will see along this section of the Muir Trail, the rugged climax to the upper South and Middle Forks of the Kings River. Each days travel will be a new venture in the high sierra grandeur.

The trail, well maintained, passes through high, open benches; across wide, open, tundra-like meadows; down deep canyons where rushing streams drown out all other sounds; beside high mountain lakes surrounded by rocky cliffs; and going over two of the loveliest passes in the Sierra — Pinchot and Mather.

The dense wooded valley at Woods Creek lies in deep contrast to the extensive open plateau below Pinchot Pass. The steep climb is rewarded by a continuous series of cascades and flowered slopes. At Pinchot Pass, to the north lies the vast basin of the headwaters of the South Fork of the Kings.

For the hearty backpacker, the untrailed islands of peaks and valleys enclosed in the Woods Creek — Kings River loop and Cartridge and Palisades creeks are sure to provide them with all the challenges of high mountains.

WOODS CREEK — GROUSE MEADOWS . . . 29.0
(via Pinchot Pass, Mather Pass, Palisade Creek)

ELEVATIONS
13,000'
12,000'
11,000'
10,000'
9,000'
8,000'
7,000'

MILES   7.0   4.5   6.0   7.5   4.0

Pinchot Pass 12,100
Mather Pass 12,050
South Fork Kings River 10,000
Palisade Lake
Palisade Creek
Middle Fork Kings River
Grouse Meadows 8,300
Simpson Meadow Trail Junction
JOHN MUIR TRAIL
Deer Meadow
Trail Junction Cartridge Creek Taboose Pass
Trail Junction Bench Lake
Trail Junction Sawmill Pass
Paradise Valley Trail Junction
Woods Creek 8,500

South Fork of the Kings River

Bill Jones, NPS

Middle Palisade Glacier   Rocky Rockwell, USFS

The back country of the Big Pine Creek Canyon is in the John Muir Wilderness. Its most outstanding feature is the Palisade Glacier some several miles beyond roads end. Typical of Sierra glaciers, it lies close up against the shaded north wall of the 14,000' Palisade Crest and is the most southerly of glaciers in the United States. At one time, during the last Ice Age, it extended down Big Pine Creek to First Bridge Campground. It is still quite active, moving in one season as much as forty feet. The milky green waters of the lakes below the glacier is evidence of its action, grinding granite boulders into fine glacial flour. In this basin lies the magnificent gentle wilderness in all its natural beauty.

Plan at least two days to make a round trip to view the glacier. Climbing the glacier requires special equipment and skills and should be attempted by only experienced climbers. Wilderness Permits are required for all trips, even for one day duration. Stream and lake fishing in the Big Pine Lakes basin is extremely good.

The only trail leading to the Muir Trail is by way of Baker and Thunder and Lightening lakes to South Lake. From there follow up Bishop Creek, crossing the divide at Bishop Pass. Dropping down across Dusy Basin it joins the Muir Trail at Little Pete Meadow in spectacular Le Conte Canyon.

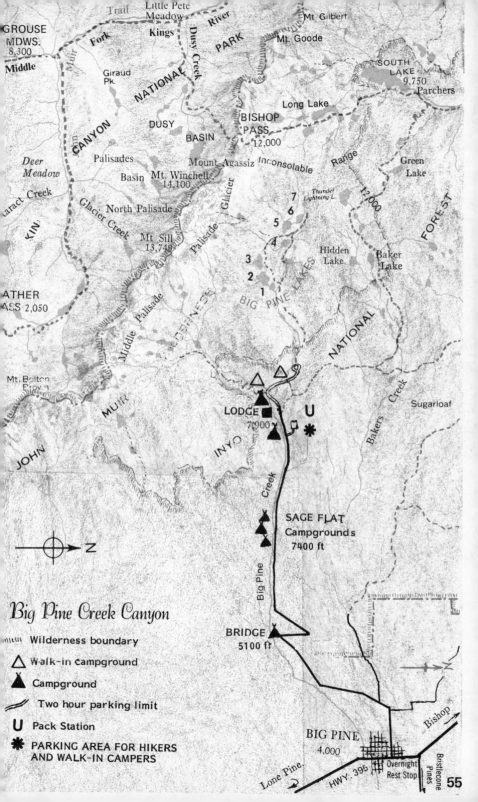

GROUSE MDWS. 8,300

Middle

Little Pete Meadow

Trail

Muir Fork

Kings

Giraud Pk.

Dusy Creek

River

Mt Gilbert

Mt Goode

SOUTH LAKE 9,750

Parchers

CANYON

NATIONAL

PARK

DUSY

BASIN

Long Lake

BISHOP PASS 12,000

Deer Meadow

Palisades

Basin

Mount Agassiz

Inconsolable

Range

Green Lake

Cataract Creek

KIN

Mt. Winchell 14,100

North Palisade

Glacier Creek

Palisade Glacier

7

6

5

4

Thunder Lightning L.

12,000

FOREST

Mt Sill 13,740

3

2

1

Hidden Lake

Baker Lake

ATHER ASS 2,050

Middle Palisade

CHINESE

BIG PINE LAKES

NATIONAL

Mt. Bolton Brown

MUIR

LODGE 7,900

U

Bakers Creek

Sugarloaf

JOHN

INYO

Big Pine Creek

SAGE FLAT Campgrounds 7400 ft

BRIDGE 5100 ft

Big Pine Creek Canyon

〜〜〜 **Wilderness boundary**

△ **Walk-in campground**

▲ **Campground**

〜 **Two hour parking limit**

U **Pack Station**

✳ **PARKING AREA FOR HIKERS AND WALK-IN CAMPERS**

BIG PINE 4,000

Bishop

Lone Pine

HWY. 395

Overnight Rest Stop

Bristlecone Pines

John Muir Pass

Of all the divide crossings in the Sierra no better choice than this was chosen to bear the name of Muir. In a region he most admired, it represents the true John Muir Sierra Country. Nearby Wanda and Helen lakes were named after Muir's two daughters.

The Muir shelter at the pass was built by the Sierra Club with the aid of the Forest Service and a generous donation by the late George Frederick Schwarz. The building's use is limited to emergency conditions only. Sudden afternoon or night storms can make the Muir Pass a difficult crossing. Its continued use and repair will depend upon the respect it is given today by the hikers who have need of it.

GROUSE MEADOW — PIUTE CREEK 29.0
(via Muir Pass, Evolution Valley)

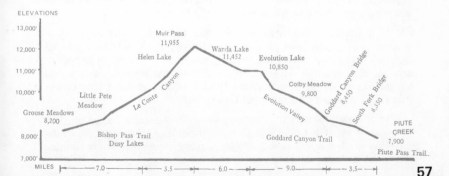

The Darwin Bench   Bill Jones, NPS

Muir Pass Country

One of the unusual contrasts of this region is its accessibility by many well developed and well used trails where hikers by the hundreds traverse the exciting north-south climax of the Muir Trail country. However, just over a ridge or up a side canyon, are scores of places almost unvisited in a whole season — some for many seasons.

It is indeed a mountaineers paradise including an array of challenging peaks, tarn spotted basins, and many deep, seldom explored canyons that carry the waters of the Kings River to the south and west, and the San Joaquin River to the north. Its eastern face is quarried by glaciers above the headwaters of Piute, Bishop and Big Pine creeks that flow northeast into the great Owens Valley.

In the early season the shaded canyon to the south can be blocked by deep snow. It is preferable to cross these snow patches early in the morning while it is still firm and always avoid snow areas where running water can be heard beneath you.

Distinctive Sierra environments are included in this region. At Grouse Meadows and Evolution Valley, open meadows are surrounded by deep, green woods. Through them flow full, sparkling, clear streams. Camping conditions are at their best including good fishing in the streams and lakes.

Approaches to the Goddard Divide crossing lead up through a succession of upper valleys and canyons enclosed by almost overwhelming canyon walls and peaks. On the south side, there is the LeConte Canyon and on the north, the Evolution basin beneath the massive Darwin range, to the east.

The actual crossing of the divide at Muir Pass (11,955') is embraced by ridges and peaks exceeding 13,000' in elevation. To the north and east are: Mt. Wallace — 13,377'; Mt. Haeckel — 13,435'; Mt. Huxley — 13,117'; Mt. Fiske — 13,524'; Mt. Darwin — 13,830'; Mt. Gilbert — 13,232'; and Mt. Thompson — 13,494'. Not to be out done by the north and east, the south and west peaks include Mt.. Goode — 13,068'; Mt. McDuffe — 13,271'; Black Giant — 13,330'; and Mt. Goddard — 13,568'. These mighty giants add their majesty as protective guardians to those who pass this way.

From this area are three unusual routes cross the country to the west:

1. Down the Middle Fork of the Kings to Tehipite Valley and out by way of Crown Valley and Wishon Reservoir.

2. Down the Kings to Simpson Meadows and over the Monarch Divide to Cedar Grove.

3.. Up Goddard Canyon over Hell-for-Sure Pass, explore the basins below the west crest of LeConte-White divides, and out by way of Wishon or Courtright reservoirs.

To the east the nearest route is by way of Dusy Basin and Bishop Pass to South Lake.

Evolution Crest — East panorama   Rocky Rockwell, USFS

60

Leave a Clean Camp
and a Dead Fire

Bishop Creek Country

Fishermen, photographers, and those who just want to sit near sparkling waters and look, will find in the upper basins of Bishop Creek a full spectrum of the wild. More than two hundred lakes lie along the eastern and western slopes of the Sierra Crest between Bishop and Piute passes. Almost half of these lakes are in the headwater basins and canyons of Bishop Creek and can be reached from road ends in a few hours.

The Upper Bishop Creek area includes a wide range of outdoor experiences from lodge, RV and camping sites to a whitebark pine nook or a cony's talus slope den. At Sabrina is a marina, coffee shop, some supplies and excellent campgrounds near the creek. There are supplies and accomodations at Cardinal Lodge on the North Fork and Habegger's Resort on the South Fork. Pack stock is available out of both North and South lakes.

The road up to South Lake is quite a pull and narrow and not recommended for large RV's. Parking and camping areas are quite limited, although there are several walk-in campgrounds for hikers.

Trailheads at Lake Sabrina lead only to the Upper Bishop Creek Basin fishing country and no exits over the range to the John Muir Trail.

At South Lake trails lead to the Upper big Pine Creek Basin or over the Bishop Pass to Dusy Basin and the Palisade country, Le Conte Canyon, Middle Fork of the Kings, and the John Muir Trail.

Trailheads at North Lake lead to the Lamarck Lakes, Piute Pass and north to the famous fishing waters of Humphrey's Basin, French Canyon, and the Bear Lakes as well as to the John Muir Trail.

Reminder: Upper Bishop Creek lies with the John Muir Wilderness, west of the divide is Kings Canyon National Park. Appropriate Wilderness Permits must be secured.

Blue Lake, Bishop Creek   Rocky Rockwell, USFS

Upper Bishop Creek

ANGLERS MAP

Adapted from materials provided by
California Department of Fish & Game
U.S. Forest Service

JOHN MUIR TRAIL

Evolution Lake

Wanda Lake

Park

National

Mt. Powell

Mt. Wallace 13377

Mt. Hoeckel 13435

Mt. Darwin 13830

Blue Heaven Lake 11,850

Hell Diver Lakes 11,750

Schober Hole Lakes

Bottleneck Lake 11,200

Fishgut Lakes 11,000

Echo Lake 11,650

Hungry Packer Lake 11,100

Midnight Lake 11,000

Dingleberry Lake 10,500

Emerald Lakes 10,450

Drunken Sailor 11,000

Topsy Turvy 10,800

Pee Wee 10,800

Sunset Lake 11,500

Moonlight Lake 11,050

Basin

Baboon Lakes 11,000

Donkey Lake 10,600

Thompson Lake 12,150

THOMPSON

Blue Lake 10,400

George Lake 10,700

Little George Lake

Kings

Canyon

Mt. Thompson 13494

Mt. Gilbert 3232

Mt. Johnson

S I E R R A

RIDGE

SOUTH LAKE

Lakes

6 11,100

5

4

3 10,300

Tyee Lakes

2

SABRINA 9000

Bishop Pass

Mt. Goode 13068

Bishop Lake 11,200

Phyllis Ledge 11,150

Spearhead Lake 10,800

Ruwau Lake 11,000

Saddlerock Lake 11,100

Timberline Tarns 11,050

Margaret Lakes 10,900

Treasure Lakes

8 11,300

7

6

5

4

3

2

1

10,646

Long Lake 10,750

Chocolate Lakes 11,100

Bull Lake 10,750

Hurd Lake 11,000

Inconsolable Lake 10,900

Mary Louise Lakes 10,650

Mule Lake 10,300

Green Lake 11,400

Brown Lake 10,750

Bluff Lake 10,500

HIKER PARKING

PARCHER'S VILLAGE 9800

RAINBOW TO LaHUPP

PACK STATION 9000

WILLOW

So

INCONSOLABLE RANGE

JOHN MUIR TRAIL

62

UPPER BISHOP CREEK LAKES

AREA	Miles from Roadend	Size in Acres	Type of Fish	Size of Fish
SOUTH LAKE				
Green Lake	1.4	17.5	RT	14"
Tyee Lake No. 4	2	11	RT	15"
Thompson	5	9.6	EB	12"
Treasure No. 1	2	12	GT	12"
Chocolate No. 1	1.5	1	EB	7"
Long Lake	1.5	29	all	17"
Saddlerock	2	30	RT	10"
Bishop Lake	2.5	25	EB	14"
SABRINA				
George L.	2	12	EB, RT	12"
Blue	1.5	30	EB, RT	16"
Sunset	3.5	29	EB	16"
Topsy Turvy	3	10	EB	8"
Moonlight	4	32	EB	12"
Hungry Packer	4	41	RT	10"
Echo	2	48	EB	10"
NORTH LAKE				
Loch Leven	1.5	10	RT, BN	10"
Upper Lamarck	1.5	15	RT, EB	12"
Piute Lake	2	19	RT, EB	10"

Five varieties of trout are found in the 83 lakes in the upper Bishop Creek area: Eastern Book — 58; Rainbow — 36; Golden — 9; Brown — 5; and Kamloops Rainbow — 3. Nearly all of the lakes are less than three hours one way from road ends at South Lake, Lake Sabrina and North Lake. With the exception of these lakes, all are above 10,000' in elevation — 40 are above 11,000' and Thompson Lake is 12,150'. Hiking at these elevations require your serious concern about your general physical condition — pace yourself accordingly.

San Joaquin River Basin

The entire region between Kings Canyon National Park at Piute Creek and the southern boundary of Yosemite National Park is administrated by the Inyo and Sierra National Forests. It is the headwater country of the San Joaquin River and has been long noted for its forests of fir and pine.

The route of the John Muir Trail between Piute Creek and Devils Postpile lies near the upper boundaries of the forest belt. This wooded region with its many small streams and meadowed basins has a correspondingly high number of birds and animals.

Between the Muir Trail and the Sierra crest lies a high, open, granite country which embraces many fine fishing lakes and streams. Highly recommended are trips into the Recesses, Pioneer Basin, and the south slope of the Silver Divide. Farther south; the East Fork, South Fork, and Hilgard branches of Bear Creek; the "Big Indian" lakes west of the Pinnacles; French Canyon and Royce Lakes; and, of course, Humphreys Basin north of the Glacier Divide.

The Izaak Waltoners, as well as the ardent photographer, will be well rewarded by a trip into any one of these places.

The area is quite accessible from road ends at Florence Lake and Lake Edison on the west and on the east side out of Bishop via Piute, Pine Creek and Italy passes. From Tom's Place; up Rock Creek, it can be reached via Mono Pass; from McGee Creek via McGee Pass and Silver Pass; or, from Mammoth Lakes, via the John Muir Trail north or south.

Trailheads lead to the Hilton Creek Lakes below Mt. Huntington and the East Fork Lakes below Broken Finger Peak. Beyond Little Lakes Valley routes lead over Morgan Pass and a good short route into Upper Mono Creek country and Pioneer Basin lakes.

PIUTE CREEK — UPPER CASCADE VALLEY 28.0
(via Seldon Pass, Quail Mdw., Silver Pass)

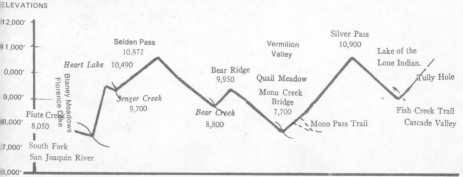

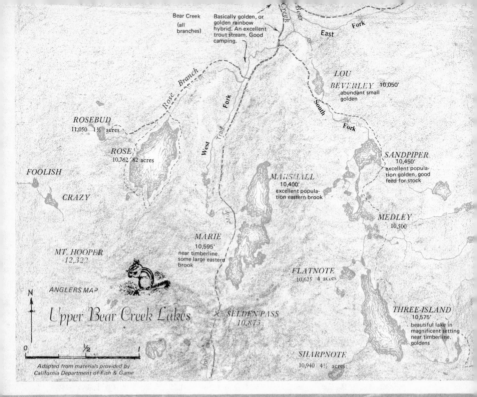

Bear Creek
(all
branches)

Basically golden, or
golden rainbow
hybrid. An excellent
trout stream. Good
camping.

East   Fork

LOU

BEVERLEY   10,050'
abundant small
golden

ROSEBUD
11,050'   1½ acres

ROSE
10,762'   82 acres

FOOLISH

CRAZY

SANDPIPER
10,450'
excellent popula-
tion golden, good
feed for stock

MARSHALL
10,400'
excellent popula-
tion eastern brook

MEDLEY
10,500

MT. HOOPER
12,322

MARIE
10,595'
near timberline
some large eastern
brook

ANGLERS MAP

Upper Bear Creek Lakes

FLATNOTE
10,625'   4 acres

THREE-ISLAND
10,575'
beautiful lake in
magnificent setting
near timberline,
goldens

N

0   ½   1

Adapted from materials provided by
California Department of Fish & Game

× SELDEN PASS
10,873

SHARPNOTE
10,940'   4½ acres

Chuck Koons

Lake Italy (Peaks L-R: Gabb, Mills, Abbot, Dade)   Chuck Koons

Of the many tributaries of the San Joaquin, the Bear Creek drainage basin is the richest in combining scenic crests, high lake-filled cirques, and great fishing situations that includes over 50 lakes and 25 miles of streams. Much of it is in or near wooded areas and meadows making camping a pleasure.

The Bear Creek drainage is a designated golden trout area. Formerly these high lakes and streams were barren. Steep cascades and waterfall barriers prevented their movement upstream. Then, in 1914 a small transfer of a few goldens were taken from their native Golden Trout Creek south of Mt. Whitney and carried into this region and planted in Marie Lake. They prospered in their new waters and spread to the streams below. Since then additional plantings have been made in other lakes suitable to their well being. In lakes where natural propagation is inadequate to maintain their numbers occasional plants by air are made. Of the 35 lakes and lakelets in this area, 26 contain golden, six with eastern brook, two with golden-rainbow hybrid, and one just rainbow.

As in most of the Sierra, bait and spinners are best where streams are high in the early season. In late summer and fall the fly fisherman will find an anglers dream come true when just as late evening shadows begin to creep across the lakes and a soft, easy, glow lights up the peaks across the basin, he makes an anxious cast near a ripple where a big one made a rise . . .   This is golden trout country for sure.

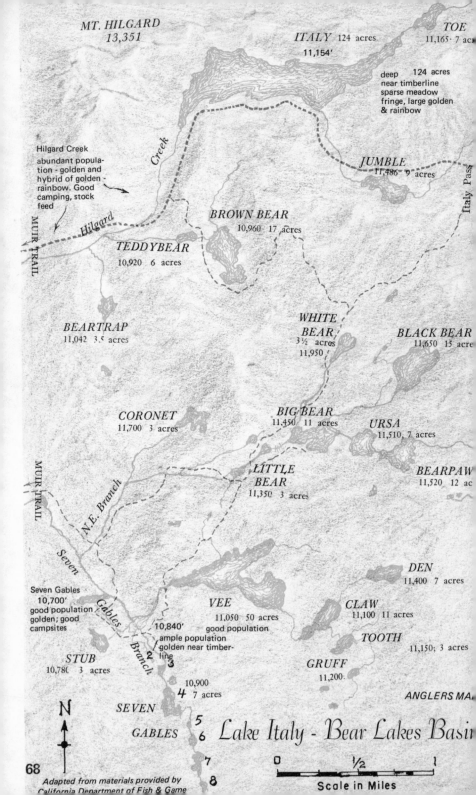

MT. HILGARD
13,351

ITALY 124 acres
11,154'

TOE
11,165· 7 ac

deep 124 acres
near timberline
sparse meadow
fringe, large golden
& rainbow

JUMBLE
11,486· 9 acres

Italy Pass

Hilgard Creek

abundant popula-
tion - golden and
hybrid of golden -
rainbow. Good
camping, stock
feed

MUIR TRAIL

Hilgard

Creek

BROWN BEAR
10,960 17 acres

TEDDYBEAR
10,920 6 acres

BEARTRAP
11,042 3.5 acres

WHITE
BEAR
3½ acres
11,950

BLACK BEAR
11,650 15 acre

CORONET
11,700 3 acres

BIG BEAR
11,450 11 acres

URSA
11,510, 7 acres

MUIR TRAIL

N.E. Branch

LITTLE
BEAR
11,350 3 acres

BEARPAW
11,520 12 ac

Seven

DEN
11,400 7 acres

Seven Gables
10,700'
good population
golden; good
campsites

Gables

CLAW
11,100 11 acres

VEE
11,050 50 acres
good population

10,840'
ample population
golden near timber-
line

TOOTH
11,150; 3 acres

STUB
10,780 3 acres

Branch

2
3

GRUFF
11,200·

10,900
4 7 acres

ANGLERS MA

N

SEVEN

GABLES

5
6

7

8

Lake Italy - Bear Lakes Basi

0   ½   1

Scale in Miles

68

Adapted from materials provided by
California Department of Fish & Game

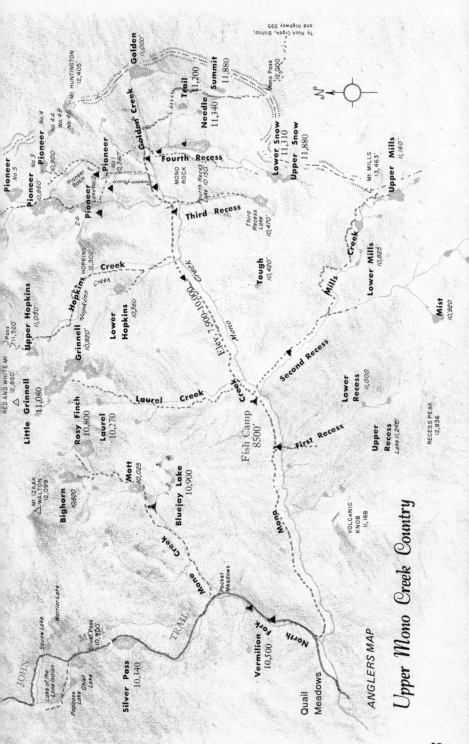

ANGLERS MAP

Upper Mono Creek Country

French Canyon

The Royce Lakes — French Canyon — Humphreys Basin area is located just north of the Kings Canyon National Park boundary. Its more than 40 square miles of high country lies entirely within the John Muir Wilderness. Seven streams and 67 lakes have been planted and managed with the idea of maintaining this region as a home for golden trout.

Most of it is above 10,000' in elevation and consequently, above timberline. Here is a rugged, granite setting where there is little or no wood for camping or feed for stock. There are no established campsites at the higher lakes. Trails are much plainer on maps than they are over the granite slopes — you will be pretty much on your own. Lower French Canyon and Hutchinson Meadow provide the best feed for stock and wood for camps. Gas stoves are needed by those making overnight trips to the upper lakes.

Lake fishing can be tricky. One day it is just great! The next day is off. These lakes lie in open basins or cirques. Their shallow, silty bottoms present conditions where reproduction is slow at best. Anglers are urged to respect not only the Fish and Game Department regulations but also their suggestions to take only what you really need and to make it really interesting, use barbless flies. If you do release fish be sure your hands are wet and there has been minimum damage to the fish.

Chuck Koons

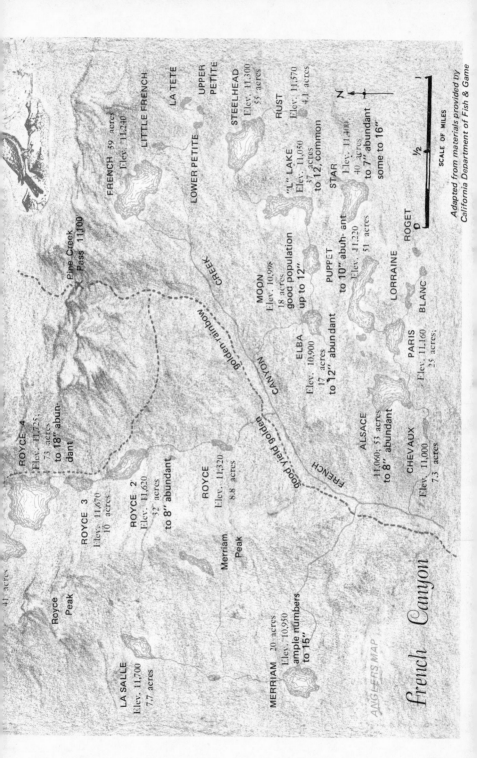

French Canyon

ANGLER'S MAP

Adapted from materials provided by
California Department of Fish & Game

SCALE OF MILES

N

½

Royce
Peak

41 acres

ROYCE 4
Elev. 11,125;
73 acres
to 18" abun-
dant

ROYCE 3
Elev. 11,670
10 acres

ROYCE 2
Elev. 11,620
32 acres
to 8" abundant

ROYCE
Elev. 11,320
8.8 acres

Merriam
Peak

LA SALLE
Elev. 11,700
7.7 acres

MERRIAM 20 acres
Elev. 10,950
ample numbers
to 15"

Pine Creek
Pass 11,100

FRENCH 59 acres
Elev. 11,240

LITTLE FRENCH

LA-TETE

UPPER
PETITE

LOWER PETITE

STEELHEAD
Elev. 11,300
55 acres

RUST
Elev. 11,570
4.1 acres

"L" LAKE
Elev. 11,050
37 acres
to 12, common

MOON
Elev. 10,998
18 acres
good population
up to 12"

golden-rainbow

CREEK

CANYON

Moquelumne

good yield golden

FRENCH

ELBA
Elev. 10,900
17 acres
to 12" abundant

STAR
Elev. 11,400;
40 acres
to 7" abundant
some to 16"

PUPPET
to 10" abun-ant
Elev. 11,220
51 acres

ROGET

LORRAINE

ALSACE
11,060; 53 acres
to 8" abundant

PARIS
Elev. 11,160
25 acres;

BLANC

CHEVAUX
Elev. 11,000
7.3 acres

Pilot Knob

DESOLATION
11,381'
14" - 20"
golden

FORSAKEN
11,500; golden

HUMPHREYS 2
11,877; golden
Eastern brook

HUMPHREYS 3
12,000'
large eastern
brooks

PIUTE PASS
11,400'

MARMOT
11,740
golden

HUMPHREYS 1
eastern brook
goldens

LOWER
DESOLATION
golden 11,150

CONY
11,480
golden

SUMMIT

MURIEL
11,320'
eastern brook
& golden trout

WEDGE
11,380
golden

MESA
11,300
golden
eastern brook

UPPER 10,820'

GOLDEN TROUT

WAHOO 1
11,180
golden

Eastern brook

LOWER
GOETHE
11,530
goldens

LOST LAKE 1
11,650

LOST LAKE 3
11,870

LOST LAKE 2
11,845

SQUARE
11,240
golden

TOMAHAWK
11,150'
golden to 14"
some eastern
brook

GOLDEN
TROUT
10,775'
3" to 9"

PACKSADDLE
10,653
Golden

WAHOO 2
11,300
golden

WAHOO 3
11,340

GOETHE
11,540'

good population

Knob
11,000

LOWER LOBE
golden

UPPER LOBE
10,900 golden

PAINE
11,020
golden

Glacier

DIVIDE

eastern brook

golden Creek

Golden

LOWER
HONEYMOON
10,440

Piute Canyon

Hutchinson Meadow

good population

Piute

French Canyon

Canyon Creek

RAMONA
10,720

UPPER
HONEYMOON
golden 10,825
plentiful to 9"

GLACIER

ANGLERS MAP

Humphreys Basin

N

0   ½   1

Westward up Pine Creek

Since early days when fishermen first came to this country the Rock Creek - Owens River has been famous. Now with Crowley Lake expanded, facilities there include water skiing. Boat rentals are available at Crowley, Rock Creek and Convict lakes.

Little Lakes Valley, Hilton Lakes or up McGee Creek are photographers delight as well as wonderful fishing country. Pack stations, camping sites, general stores, lodging and meals are at Crowley Lake, Rock Creek, Tom's Place, Convict Lake and McGee Creek.

74

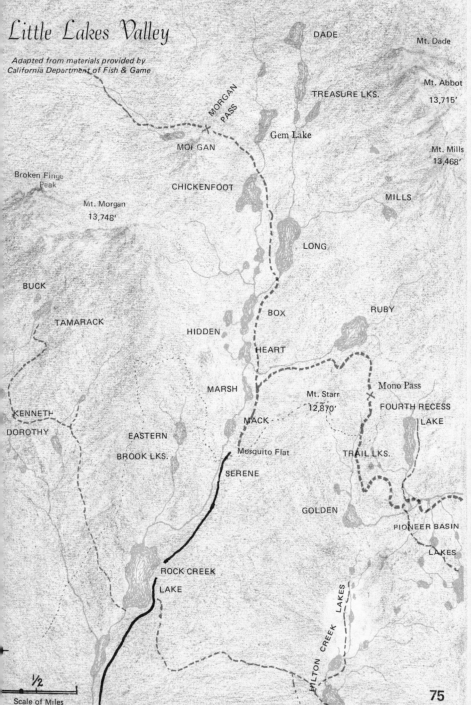

ANGLERS MAP

Little Lakes Valley

Adapted from materials provided by
California Department of Fish & Game

Bear Creek Spire

SPIRE

DADE

Mt. Dade

Mt. Abbot
13,715'

TREASURE LKS.

MORGAN PASS

Gem Lake

Mt. Mills
13,468'

MORGAN

CHICKENFOOT

MILLS

Broken Finger Peak

Mt. Morgan
13,748'

LONG

BUCK

BOX

RUBY

TAMARACK

HIDDEN

HEART

MARSH

Mono Pass

KENNETH

Mt. Starr
12,870'

FOURTH RECESS
LAKE

DOROTHY

MACK

EASTERN

Mosquito Flat

TRAIL LKS.

BROOK LKS.

SERENE

GOLDEN

PIONEER BASIN

LAKES

ROCK CREEK

LAKE

HILTON CREEK LAKES

½

Scale of Miles

75

Barney Lake   Rocky Rockwell, USFS

All too many hikers passing through this region do so with an anticipation of what is ahead rather than considering it as a destination in itself. Northbound hikers along the Muir Trail are anxiously awaiting the re-supply services at Reds Meadow or Mammoth. Southbound earthlings hurry to reach the Evolution Valley, glacial divides, and high passes to the south.

Some of the finest camping experiences in the Sierra are found in this broad, wooded basin of the headwaters of the San Joaquin. The plethora of water and forest life here covers a wide range in such places as Margaret Lakes, Fish Creek — Cascade Valley, large lakes above the Muir Trail along the southwestern slopes of Mammoth Crest, and Mono Creek headwaters bying between Silver and Mono Divides.

The very place names give rise to invite their exploration: Sharktooth Peak, Rainbow Lake, Devils Bathtub, Lake of the Lone Indian, and Bighorn or Rosy Finch lakes.

UPPER CASCADE VALLEY — DEVILS POSTPILE 19.5
(via Tully Hole, Virginia Lake)

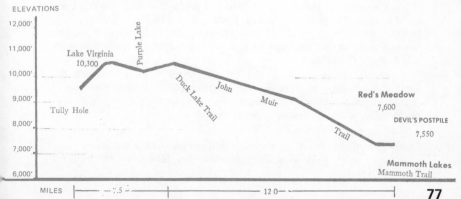

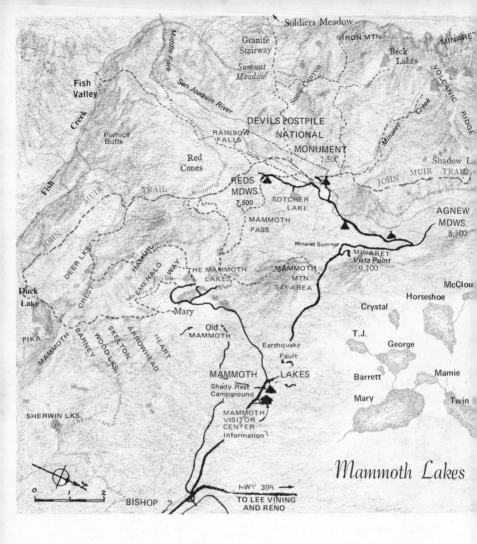

Mammoth Lakes

Activities in the Mammoth Lakes area includes much more than winter sports or a trip to the Devils Postpile in summer. They include the exploration of the unusual remains of geologic volcanic action such as the Inyo Craters, Obsiderian Dome, and the Earthquake Fault. Great panoramic views of the adjacent desert basins to the east and the Ritter Range to the west can be seen from summits of Black Mountain and Lookout Mountain.

In the evening, go to the Minaret Vista Point and watch the setting sun behind the craggy Minarets across the valley! Few places provide such a sublime experience or such a sweeping contrast of lush green valley with the towering crests above.

Mammoth Lake Trailheads:
Duck Lake Trail: From Coldwater Campground this trail leads to Barney Lake, Duck Lake and junctions with the John Muir-Pacific Crest Trail. (6.0 miles)

Pika and Duck Lakes from Duck Pass   Rocky Rockwell, USFS

Mammoth Crest Trail: From Lake George trail makes steep climb west to Mammoth Crest, follows along the crest for five miles, past Deer Lakes, Duck Lake and junctions with John Muir-Pacific Crest Trail. (10 miles)

Mammoth Pass Trails: From Horseshoe/McCloud lakes trail leads south and junctions with Muir Trail below Red Cone (3.5 miles) or leads west from Mammoth Pass to Reds Meadow (5.0 miles) and junctions with Muir Trail and Old Mammoth Trail leading into upper San Joaquin.

For a trip to Summit Meadow (6.0 miles, one-day or overnight trip) follow the old Indian and pioneer trans-Sierra trail. It is here that Governor Reagan and scores of devoted conservationists held the landmark meeting declaring the whole region — Minaret Wilderness, which Congress defines as an area where the earth and its community of life are untrammeled by man, where man himself is a visitor who does not remain. It is to stay permanently in its natural setting without the intrusion of structures or new roads. It is an action to draw the line on development which inevitably leads to the disappearance of our wilderness.

Incidentally, this action settled once and for all the reoccuring efforts by some groups to develop a road across the Sierra in this region. Also this is why the road into the Postpile and Reds Meadow is unimproved. It is maintained as a graded dirt road and never will be paved.

Russ Johnson

The formation of the Devils Postpile has undergone several definite stages over many centuries. It is of volcanic origin and had its beginnings in the great earthquake fault that lies along the east side of the Sierra range. Weaknesses along this fracture allowed great flows of lava to pour forth, some to 1,000' in depth.

As these flows cooled off, their uniformity of material and temperature caused an evenness of stress on the surface of the shrinking lava. Cracks, in geometric patterns, developed in much the same way as they do in mud flats when they dry up. These cracks joined together, forming four to seven sided units 20''' to 30'' in diameter. As the cooling process continued, the cracking changed from horizontal action on the surface to vertical action downward to the base of the flow, forming huge columns or "posts."

In subsequent geologic eras the glaciers passed over this region, cutting down the thickness of the lava flows, and tore away whole sections, leaving exposed the sheer columns of basalt. The evidences of this glacial action are still seen in the great pile of posts below the formation and the polished surbace of the tops of many sections still standing.

Devils Postpile

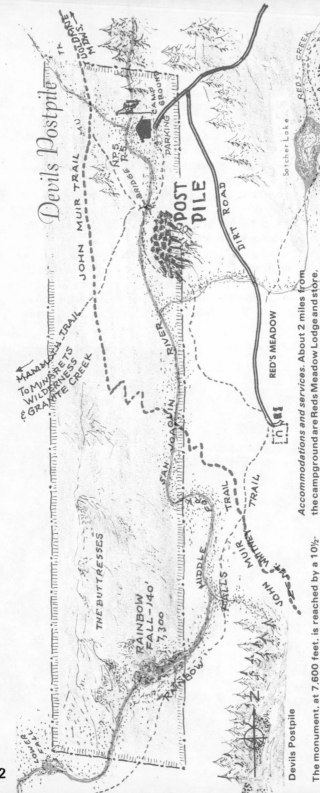

Devils Postpile

Devils Postpile

The monument, at 7,600 feet, is reached by a 10½-mile drive to Minaret Summit on a paved road from U.S. 395, then by 7 miles of unpaved mountain road.

In summer, park rangers are on duty to help visitors and to conduct naturalist activities. If you need information or are in any difficulty, see a park ranger.

Accommodations and services. About 2 miles from the campground are Reds Meadow Lodge and store, where gasoline, oil, groceries, meals, cabins, mail service, and saddle and pack horses are available.

Camping. Near the park ranger station a campground is maintained from about June 15 to October 1, depending upon the weather.

Fishing is permitted in the monument, but hunting is forbidden. A California angling license is required for persons 16 years of age or over.

Minarets Wilderness

From a half dozen campgrounds, trailheads invite the exploration of the valley, streams and falls, geological formations at the Postpile, and the high lakes lying along the rugged slope of the Ritter Range.

To see the Rainbow Falls or the Postpile, it is an easy one-half day walk along the Middle Fork of the San Joaquin.

From the Devils Postpile trailhead at the north boundary several routes lead to almost a hundred lakes for a one-day or overnight trip. The waters of this area are presently stocked with Eastern brook, golden and rainbow trout.

SNOW CANYON — BECK LAKES

Good fishing and camping conditions are found along Kings Creek and the upper lakes. At Upper Beck Lake wood is scarce so plan accordingly. This trip can be an extension to that of Summit Meadow and would make a good loop trip that includes many of the lakes.

MINARET CREEK — MINARET LAKE

This is a most unusual setting to enjoy the full magnitude of the majestic Minarets. Good fishing here. Take your camera and plenty of film. Iceberg Lake is well named due to the presence of ice floating in the lake well into the summer.

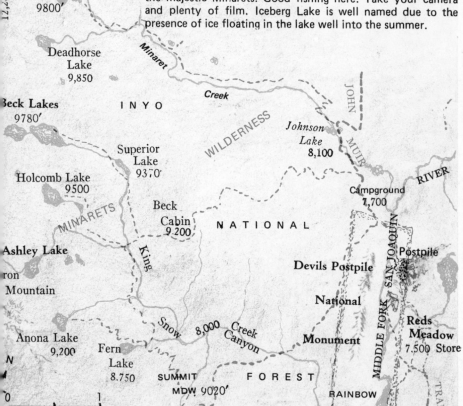

ydiver
Lakes 10,400

iza Lake
9300'

erg Lake
800'

Cecile Lake
10,300

Minaret
Lakes
9800'

12,300

Deadhorse
Lake
9,850

Minaret

Creek

Beck Lakes
9780'

INYO

WILDERNESS

JOHN

Johnson
Lake
8,100

MUIR

Superior
Lake
9370'

RIVER

Holcomb Lake
9500

Campground
7,700

MINARETS

Beck
Cabin
9,200

NATIONAL

Ashley Lake

King

Postpile

ron
Mountain

Devils Postpile

MIDDLE FORK OF SAN JOAQUIN

National

Reds
Meadow
7,500 Store

Anona Lake
9,200

Fern
Lake
8,750

Snow

8,000

Creek
Canyon

Monument

SUMMIT
MDW 9020'

FOREST

RAINBOW

TRAIL

N

FALLS
7,360

0   1

Scale of Miles

Minarets Country

Tuolumne Meadows

Mt. McCLURE

DONOHUE PASS
11,050

Gem Lake

Agnew Lake

Rush Creek

MT. LYELL

Waugh Lake

AGNEW PASS

SAN JOAQUIN MTN

Marie Lake

Island Pass

Yosemite Valley

NATIONAL PARK

RODGERS PEAK

Thousand Island Lake

Garnet Lake

YOSEMITE

Lyell Fork

Merced River

MT. DAVIS
12,308

BANNER PEAK
12,957

Shadow Lake

San Joaquin River

PACIFIC CREST TRAIL

ELECTRA PEAK

Twin Island Lakes
9600'

RITTER

RITTER PEAK
13,156

JOHN MUIR TRAIL

Wilderness

FOERSTER PEAK
12,059

BENCH CANYON
10,00

Stevenson Meadow

VOLCANIC RIDGE

Agnew Meadow

Harriet Lake
10,300

San Joaquin Divide

LONG MTN.

Hemlock Crossing

Minaret Creek

MINARETS RANGE

ISBERG PASS
10,500

Minarets

Long Creek

Dike Creek

Beck Lakes

DEVILS POSTPILE
7,550

Merced

POST PEAK PASS
10,600

SADLER PEAK
10,562

Iron Creek

Iron

IRON MTN.
11,149

Summit Meadow
9,000

King Creek

POST PEAK TRAIL

East Fork

Cora Lakes

NORTH FORK

Lily Lake

Granite Stairway
9,200

MAMMOTH

RAINBOW

Post Creek

TIMBER KNOB
9,963

Creek

"77" CORRAL

GREEN MTN.
8,600'

Sheep Crossing
6,100

Snake Mdw.
7,100'

CARGYL MD ?
8,00

West Fork

GRANITE

POSTPILE

SAN JOAQUIN

Cargyle Creek

Stairway Creek

SAN JOAQUIN RIVER

Fish Creek

Granite Creek
Campground
7,000

SOLDIER MEADOW
7,000

MIDDLE FORK

N

CLOVER MEADOW
7,000

Creek

CATTLE MTN.
7,915

JUNCTION BUTTE 6,570

MILLER CROSSING

JUNCTION BLUFFS

The great basin of the North Fork of the San Joaquin is more remote and less frequently visited than the area between Granite Creek and the south boundary country of Yosemite National Park. It is a rugged, above timberline environment with only a minimum number of trails. You will be pretty much on your own here. It is bounded on the west by the Long Mountain — Sadler Peak Ridge averaging above 10,500', and on the east by the magnificent Ritter Range. This is truly an appropriate setting for a wilderness area.

Entries into this region can be made from the east via Reds Meadow/Devils Postpile, and from the west via Bass Lake on the Pines — Beasore Road or North Fork via the Minarets Road to Clover Meadow and Granite Creek. Supplies can be secured at all these places, saddle and pack stock are available at Reds Meadow and Miller Meadow.

The best fishing is usually found in the river, or in Twin Island, Blue or Rockbound lakes. For general fishing in the Minaret Wilderness, the lakes and streams in the Granite Creek basin are the most productive. You can obtain your Wilderness Permit at Clover Meadow or the North Fork Ranger Station. (District Ranger, Minarets District, North Fork, CA, 93463)

Caution: Climbing in the Minarets should be done only by well equipped and experienced climbers, and never alone.

Clyde Minaret   Rocky Rockwell, USFS

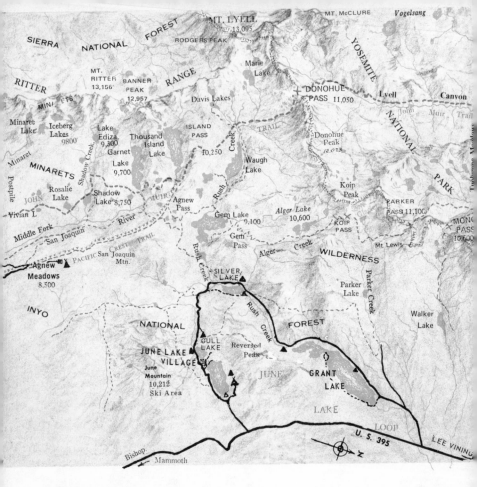

June Lake Loop

In winter June lake is a mecca for winter sports to people and in summer there is a wide variety of camping activities. Accommodations include stores, lodges and several trailer parks and campgrounds along the lake shore. Trails out of June Lake lead to Mammoth, the Thousand Island and Rush Creek basins and north to Tuolumne Meadows via Koip Peak and Parker Pass.

For hearty backpackers looking for the unusual, there is a very interesting but seldom used alternate route between Agnew Meadows and Tuolumne Meadows. Follow the valley trail along the San Joaquin River, or the new Pacific Crest Trail route along the high canyon rim up to the Badger Lakes area. From there continue by way of Gen Lake, Gem Pass, Alger Lake, Kiop Peak Pass, Kiop Glacier, Parker Pass and Dana Meadows.

This is a rough, undeveloped route. When traveling it some 30 years ago I swore it had been laid out by a lost mountain sheep. From what I hear, it is little better today. Check on this carefully when getting your Wilderness Permit. (Note: Usually no camping in the Dana Meadows — Parker Creek area as this is Tuolumne's water supply.)

June Lake   Russ Johnson

In winter it is a glorious sight to watch the development of great snow banners off these peaks as windstorms sweep up over their crests carrying great streams of powdery snow far out over the valleys to the east.

Island Pass marks the parting of the waters flowing west down the San Joaquin and those from the east slope of Lyell, Donohue and Kiop crests. Rush Creek flowing east, pauses awhile, at Gem and Agnew lakes before its confluence with Reverse Creek near Silver Lake. These waters flow north to Mono Lake.

From the Pass it is but a short distance out along the ridge to Donohue Peak (12,073'). From there can be seen the desert basins and the Basin Ranges far to the east. Careful exploration to the west toward Mt. Lyell (13,114') brings a closer view of the glacier.

Mt. Lyell is the apex of the Cathedral-Ritter Range and the Donohue-Foerster Crest. Streams flow south to the San Joaquin, east into the desert basin at Owens Lake, west to the Merced River and on down through Yosemite Valley, and north down the Grand Canyon of the Tuolumne.

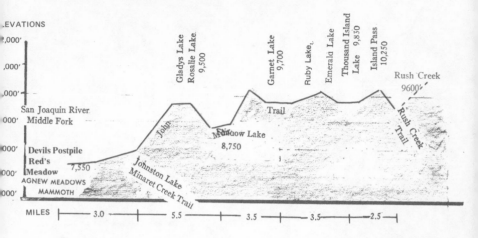

The John Muir Trail has always been associated with a high country experience. The route followed in this basin between the Minarets and the South Fork of the San Joaquin is an exception. True, the biggest part of it is barren due to its high elevation and glaciated rock floor. However, where conditions are favorable, there are good groves of lodgepole pine, Jeffrey pine, red fir, and mountain hemlock. Near streams in the lower valleys are willows and poplar.

There is a unique geological feature here that determined the location of the only part of the John Muir Trail that lies east of the Sierra Crest. The magnificant Cathedral-Ritter Range complex ends at Iron Mountain (11,149'). To the south, elevations drop off rapidly into the Fish Valley trough. The Sierra Nevada Crest has now moved eastward. Its beginnings lie in the San Joaquin Mountain (11,600') — Mammoth Mountain (11,051) chain that soon develops into the Mammoth and Sierra Nevada Crest where elevations begin to exceed 12,000' and 13,000'. The break in the Sierra chain provides the setting for the only major stream of the Sierra that rises east of the main crest and flows west to the Pacific.

Parallel to the John Muir Trail are two routes — one along the river connecting with trails to the high lakes and the other the new Pacific Crest Trail. From Agnew Meadows the Pacific Crest Trail has been completed between the Postpile and Donohue Pass.

From near Minaret Falls it follows north along the San Joaquin to Agnew Meadows. Here it ascends the east valley wall via switchbacks for about a mile and then follows a panoramic contour route to the Badger Lakes. Turning west it joins the John Muir Trail at the lower end of Thousand Island Lake and continues north to Rush Creek, Donohue Pass and Tuolumne Meadows. Several different loop trips can be planned to include Shadow, Garnet, Thousand Island and upper Rush Creek lakes. It is approximately ten miles between Agnew Meadows and the lower end of Thousand Island.

From Agnew Meadows to Lake Ediza (7 miles; all-day trip) the route follows up the San Joaquin to Olaine Lake, then turns west to cross the river and follows Shadow Creek to its source in Cecile, Iceberg, Nydiver and Ediza lakes.

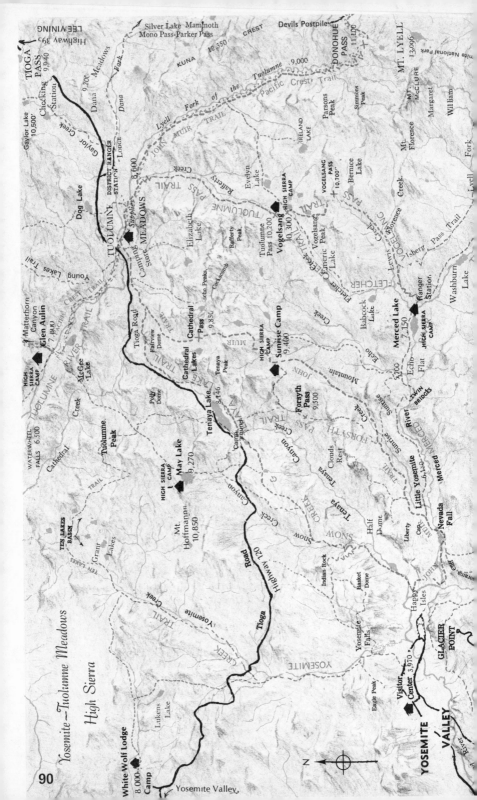

Yosemite—Tuolumne Meadows
High Sierra

90

Lake Ediza

Jim Kirschenrner
USFS

Some of the grandest scenery of the Sierra is found in the sett ig of the Muir Trail between Tuolumne Meadows and the Postpile. The beginnings of the San Joaquin gather the waters from Shadow, Garnet and Thousand Island lakes and provide an enticing setting for reflection of Banner and Ritter peaks in the late afternoon.

The Donohue Pass crossing is great! To those headed south there is an enticing glimpse of the grand things to come far down the Sierra Crest. To those headed north the panoramic scene reaches down the ever extending canyons where headwaters of the Tuolumne River lie.

It is indeed a moving experience to sit out on a starlit night in the shelter of a great rock here in this pass and listen to the noisy waters of streams far below. From glacial tarns and terminal moraines, they carry the milky white glacial flour — evidence of their continuing reduction of these granite ranges. John Muir, in recalling a visit to this region expressed it well when he gazed down upon the "giant mountains, valleys innumerable, glaciers and meadows, rivers and lakes, with the wide blue sky bent tenderly over then all, —— in contemplation of natures methods of landscape creation."

RUSH CREEK – TUOLUMNE MEADOWS 19.5
(via Donohue Pass, Lyell Fork Canyon)

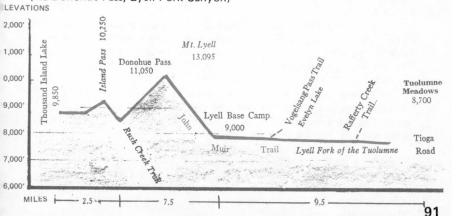

91

TUOLUMNE MEADOWS Gerald Born, NPS

In all the Sierra Nevada there is only one Tuolumne Meadows. The deep meadows, more than a mile wide below the campground, extends some eight miles up canyon and almost three miles down canyon. In this broad, almost flat meadow there is less than 500 feet difference in elevation between the lower and upper ends.

Tuolumne Meadows marks the division point of the Pacific Crest and the John Muir trails. Turning west, the Muir Trail follows the watershed of the Merced into Yosemite Valley while the Pacific Crest Trail goes north to the Park boundary at Dorothy Lake.

Services include Lodge, store, pack station, gas station, post office and a large campground. Strategically located at the hub of the Yosemite High Sierra on the Tioga Pass Road, it has become the outfitting place for trails into the back country. The Wilderness Permit Kiosk is near the District Ranger Station where they will also help

92 plan your trip.

John Muir Trail

The song of birds, the noisy, tumbling waters, and being sorrounded by three thousand foot canyon walls, is a most joyous beginning for backcountry trips.

It is a long, three and a half miles to the top of Nevada Fall. Those with heavy packs will do well to stick to the main trail where the higher route gives broader views of the canyon and the long switchbacks require less effort than the steep, and at places very wet, Mist Trail below Vernal Fall.

YOSEMITE VALLEY – TUOLUMNE MEADOWS....23.5
(via Sunrise Mountain, Cathedral Pass)

Cathedral Peak

Ralph Anderson, NPS

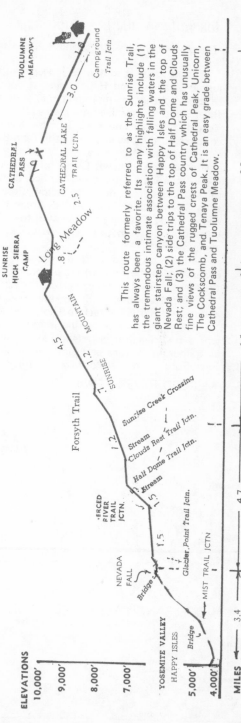

This route formerly referred to as the Sunrise Trail, has always been a favorite. Its many highlights include (1) the tremendous intimate association with falling waters in the giant stairstep canyon between Happy Isles and the top of Nevada Fall; (2) side trips to the top of Half Dome and Clouds Rest; and (3) the Cathedral Pass country which has unusually fine views of the rugged crests of Cathedral Peak, Unicorn, The Cockscomb, and Tenaya Peak. It is an easy grade between Cathedral Pass and Tuolumne Meadow.

93

Yosemite Valley - Tuolumne Meadows

The Merced River — Vogelsang Route

This route is somewhat longer than the Muir Trail between Tuolumne Meadows and Happy Isles. It does, however, make a most satisfactory change of mountain trail as it follows close to the Merced River from Happy Isles to Merced Lake. The forested upper Little Yosemite Valley and deep woodsy feeling at Lost Valley are great contrasts to the cascades above the Twin Bridges crossing.

Between Merced Lake to Vogelsang two routes present different enviroments. The Lewis Creek route passes trails to some half dozen lakes including Florence and Bernice, then makes an easy ascent to Vogelsang Pass, drops down to follow close to Vogelsang Lake and the High Sierra Camp. The Fletcher Creek trail provides fine lake fishing and camping. Passing to the west of towering Vogelsang Peak (11,511') you may be fortunate enough to see an eagle soaring in the updraft along the cliffs.

Time taken to make the ascent to Vogelsang Peak will be most rewarding, in the far reaching panorama of the many eastern basins of the Merced River and north across the vast watershed of the Tuolumne.

From Vogelsang it is an easy down grade trip across open tundra country via Rafferty Creek to Tuolumne.

A more varied offering is found on the Evelyn Lake alternate where trails lead up to Ireland Lake. You can cross country along the east slope of Parsons and Simmons peak where fine views down the Lyell Fork and into the deep glacier filled cirques of McClure and Lyell.

MERCED RIVER TRAIL

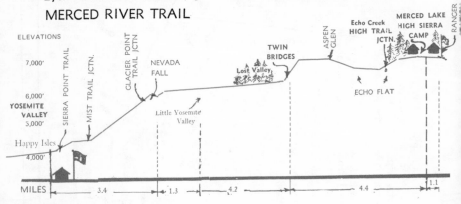

VOGELSANG PASS TRAIL

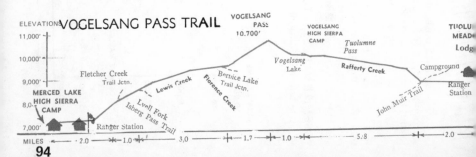

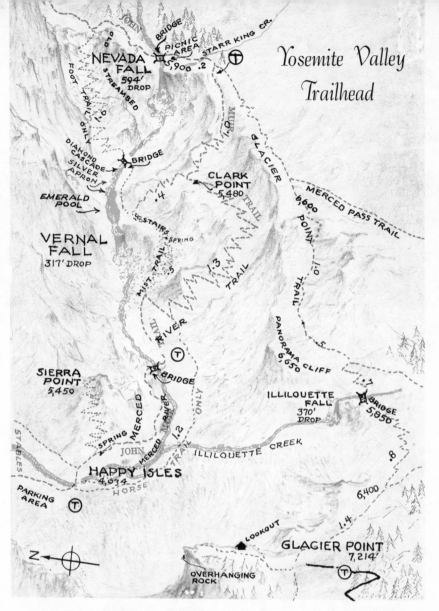

Yosemite Valley
Trailhead

The Incomparable Valley always has been the gathering place of those seeking association with the High Sierra. Ever since John Muir sought the answer to Yosemite's glacial origins, trails into the back-country have been developed. At first the deep, almost impenetrable valley was reluctant to accept more than a handful of visitors other than the Indians who used it as a wintering place where acorns, fish, and game were plentiful.

Trail building in such country was slow in developing. It took the persistant care of wilderness lovers (and a lot of dynamite) to get by the great stairstep falls and beyond the canyon walls. Today, more than a thousand miles of trails reach out into remote areas. Well maintained and signed, they are patrolled during the summer by rangers.

Tenaya Lake   Ralph Anderson, NPS

OTHER ROUTES FROM YOSEMITE VALLEY TO TUOLUMNE MEADOWS

As an answer to the complaints that many make about the crowded trails, two extended trips that are less traveled, have beautiful camping and lakes to fish are offered for your consideration here. As the Buck Camp ranger said to us last summer, "it was so lonesome out here, I had no one to talk to but my horse!"

One good long trip would be the grand tour of the South Boundary country. Explore the Illilouette basin, Clark Range and Triple Divide country, then follow the old Isberg Pass trail north to Lewis Creek, cross Vogelsang Pass and continue to Tuolumne.

A second route includes the best of the spectacular North Country region. Follow up Yosemite Creek basin above Yosemite Falls and proceed to Pate Valley by way of White Wolf and Harden Lake. From Pate Valley enjoy the Grand Canyon of the Tuolumne, through the Muir Gorge, past Waterwheel Falls, Glen Aulin and on to Tuolumne.

TENAYA LAKE TRAIL (25 miles)

This is the shortest route between Tuolumne Meadows and Yosemite Valley. It follows the north shoulder of Tenaya Canyon and its tributary, Snow Creek. Its highlights include the Tenaya Lake valley, views across canyon of the tremendous exposed granite slope of Clouds Rest, and quite unusual views of Yosemite Valley along its north rim near Indian Rock and Basket Dome.

For those planning trips in the more remote areas of the Park and wish to avoid the overcrowded valley as well as the long, steep climb up canyon wall switchbacks, general supplies and pack stock are available at Wawona, Mather, White Wolf, and Tuolumne Meadows.

For complete coverage of all the trails in Yosemite National Park, see our companion volume, "Yosemite Trails."

96

Middle Fork of the Kings

Along the South and Middle Forks of the Kings there is a concentration of domes, sheer granite walls and deep U-shaped canyons that excels in area and variety anything else in the Sierra.

Muir's writings of the South Fork describe it as

" . . . a yet greater valley . . . above the most extensive groves and forests of the Giant Sequoia, and beneath the highest mountains in the Sierra where the canyons are deepest and the snow-laden peaks are crowded most closely together . . . "

The Middle Fork of the Kings is a place set apart in remoteness and grandeur. Tehipite Dome stands more than 3,000' above the valley. Its unusual form with its sheer face is one of the most striking domes of the Sierra. From Tehipite Valley to its source in the Palisade Crest and upper LeConte Canyon, the Middle Fork waters draw from such outstanding places as the Crown Valley, the Monarch Divide, the Cirque Crest, Palisade Basin, LeConte Canyon, Blue Canyon, and the Tunemah-Goddard Creek country. The towering peaks, cascades and waterfalls are breathtaking in size and beauty.

From Tehipite Valley to Muir Pass trails follow along close to the river in a continuous experience of roaring, tumbling waters surrounded by overwhelming granite walls. In charming relief to all this ruggedness are the lovely flowered meadows at Simpson, Grouse and Little Pete.

Tehipite Dome   Middle Fork of the Kings Canyon   National Park Service

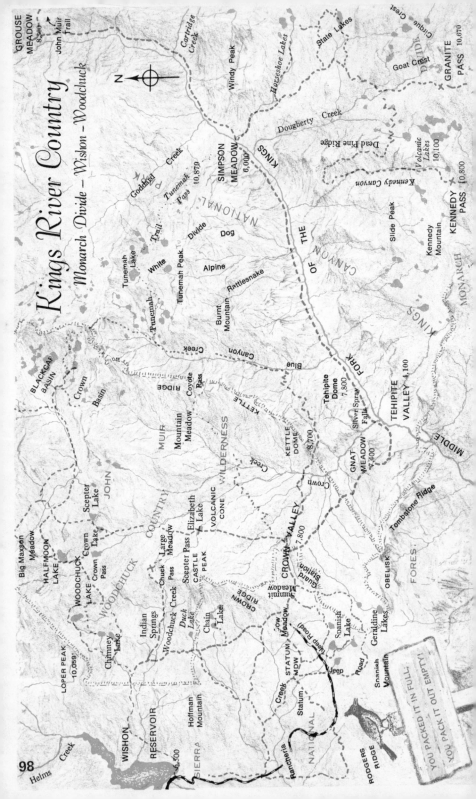

Sierra Forest Trails

The Sierra is a friendly place inviting entry at all seasons. Its extensive, striking geology along the high eastern crest has, since early days, excited the interest of scholars and mountaineers. For decades the goal of vacationers has been the High Sierra. The term has become synonymous with any place in the mountains above the oak tree and digger pine belt. The almost revered regard Californians have had about this granite crest has created a problem of serious magnitude as visitations increased from a few hundred a year to several million during a single summer.

A recent house count taken shows that on any given day in July or August as many as nine to ten thousand people are backpacking in the wilderness areas along the John Muir-Pacific Crest trail. This is Wilderness?

Strangely enough this corridor region named to give honor to John Muir traverses an area he seldom visited. Most of his journeys were an up canyon - down canyon course exploring the rivers and their source. He was no yodeling mountaineer seeking peaks to climb. His true love was the entire wilderness. Of special concern to him were the deep grassy valleys and meadows that supported a complete spectrum of wildlife. If he were here today we seriously question if he would bother making a complete trip on the trail that bears his name.

This Sierra Forest trail section hopefully reflects an alternative attitude toward the use of the Sierra for backcountry trips. It includes the great forest covered belt between Sequoia and the Emigrant Basin north of Yosemite National Park. It lies along the west slope of the mountains where rain, snow, and deep soil have developed an abundance of trees, streams, and wildlife. Some five thousand square miles in area, its size and woodland character has been long utilized by lumbermen but all too seldom considered as a vacation land.

Some of the finest camping country in North America is here in this area. It is easily accessible with lots of wood, water and could accommodate double the number of people with little or no harm to the enviroment. The very character of this country provides it with a recovery ability to withstand the impact of vast numbers of visitors.

WISHON RESERVOIR — SIMPSON MEADOW 35.0
(via Crown Valley, Gnat Meadow)

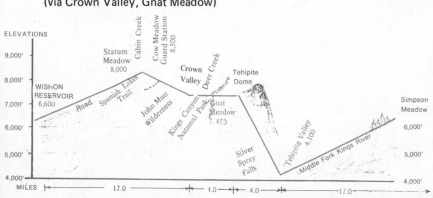

Fin Dome from Upper Geraldine Lake   Ben Flanagan, USFS

Between Tehipite Valley on the Kings and the south boundary of Yosemite National Park are the drainage basins of the Middle and North Fork of the Kings and the San Joaquin rivers. Its average elevation and exposure on the Sierra slope provides it with a climatic condition especially suited to forest and wildlife.

Access to this region can be made at:

1. <u>Sanger:</u> To Pine Flat Reservoir, Balch Camp and Black Rock Station and Wishon Reservoir. This is a long, winding road and is probably the least desirable of the access routes available.

2. <u>Clovis:</u> To Shaver Lake, Dinkey Creek, and Wishon Reservoir. This is a very good surfaced road that now extends above Wishon to Courtright Reservoir.

3. <u>Shaver Lake to Huntington Lake</u>: Several routes run south east to the Courtright Reservoir. (Good road all the way in.) Trails lead into the North Fork of the Kings and Blackcap Basin.

4. <u>Huntington Lake to Florence Lake</u>: Trailheads lead south to the North Fork of the Kings, via Mosquito Pass and Thompson Pass, east to the Muir Trail at Blayney Meadows and northeast to Upper Bear Creek Lakes and Humphreys Basin.

5. <u>Huntington Lake to Lake Edison</u>: Trailheads lead south to upper Bear Creek and Humphreys Basin, east to the Mono Creek-Recess country and north to the Devils Bathtub, Graveyard Lakes, Margaret Lakes and Cascade Valley on Fish Creek.

6. <u>Pine Creek Roadend</u> (10 miles west of HWY 395) Routes lead over Pine Creek pass into French Canyon, down Piute Creek to the junction with the San Joaquin, up Goddard Canyon, Hell-For-Sure Pass and Red Mountain Basin. From there trails along the North Fork of the Kings and cross country routes extend south into Bench Valley, Blackcap and Crown basins.

Trans-Sierra routes beginning at Wishon/Courtright or Pine Creek include some of the finest scenic, camping and good fishing and, in general, it is much less traveled than the country adjacent to the John Muir Trail.

101

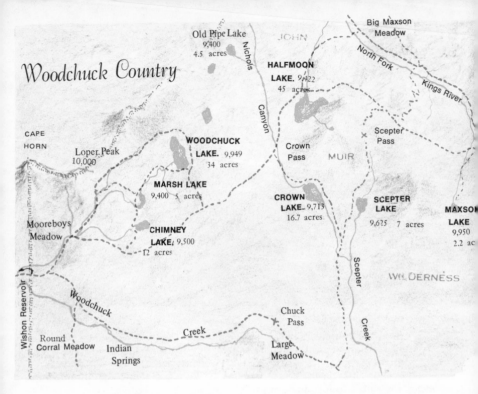

Woodchuck Country

Old Pipe Lake
9,400
4.5 acres

JOHN

Big Maxson
Meadow

North Fork

HALFMOON
LAKE. 9,422
45 acres

Kings River

Nichols

Canyon

CAPE
HORN

Loper Peak
10,000

**WOODCHUCK
LAKE.** 9,949
34 acres

Crown
Pass

MUIR

Scepter
Pass

Mooreboys
Meadow

MARSH LAKE
9,400 5 acres

**CHIMNEY
LAKE** 9,500
12 acres

**CROWN
LAKE.** 9,713
16.7 acres

**SCEPTER
LAKE**

9,625 7 acres

**MAXSON
LAKE**
9,950
2.2 ac

WILDERNESS

Scepter

Wishon Reservoir

Woodchuck

Creek

Chuck
Pass

Round
Corral Meadow

Indian
Springs

Large
Meadow

Creek

Halfmoon Lake

Ben Flanagan, USFS

Woodchuck Lake   Ben Flanagan, USFS

From the Wishon Dam the route is a continuous eight mile climb all the way to Woodchuck. The entire region welcomes camping with its gentle, partly forested hills, and meadow-bordered lakes. To the south and east is found some of the finest stands of lodgepole pine, mountain hemlock, and red and white fir. Here and there partially bare ridges lend contrast to the deep green woods and blue skies. Fishing is quite good.

Woodchuck Lake, nestled in between two almost bald ridges has meadows above and below it and supports a good size Eastern book. The smaller Marsh and Chimney lakes, at slightly lower elevations, also carry brooks. At head of Scepter Creek the meadow rimmed Crown Lake produces rainbow. Good stream fishing is found in Woodchuck and Scepter creeks that carry rainbow and Eastern brook. North of Woodchuck Lake in Old Pipe Lake, good size rainbow are abundant.

WISHON RESERVOIR — GODDARD CANYON BRIDGE 34.5
(via Woodchuck Lake, Halfmoon Lake, Big Maxon Meadow, Bench Valley)

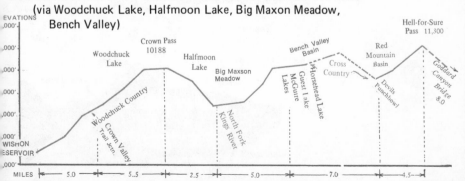

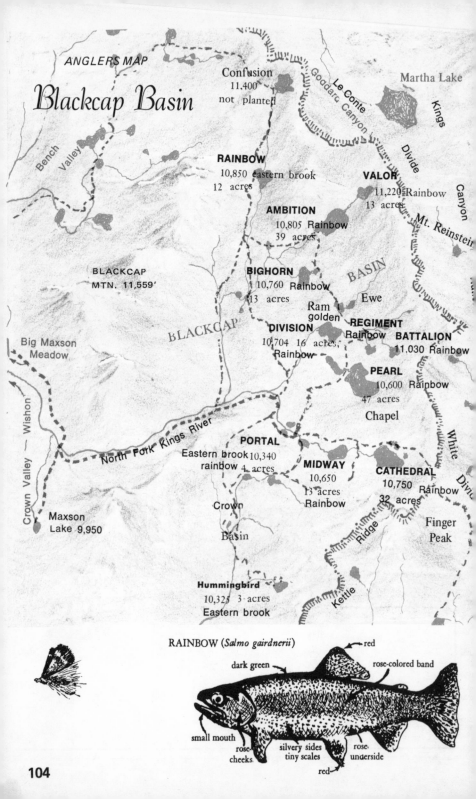

ANGLERS MAP

Blackcap Basin

Confusion
11,400
not planted

Le Conte

Martha Lake

Goddard Canyon

Kings

Bench Valley

Divide

RAINBOW
10,850 eastern brook
12 acres

VALOR
11,220 Rainbow
13 acres

AMBITION
10,805 Rainbow
39 acres

Canyon

Mt. Reinstein

BLACKCAP
MTN. 11,559'

BIGHORN
10,760 Rainbow
13 acres

BASIN

Ewe

Ram
golden

REGIMENT
Rainbow

BATTALION
11,030 Rainbow

BLACKCAP

DIVISION
10,704 16 acres
Rainbow

Big Maxson
Meadow

PEARL
10,600 Rainbow
47 acres

Chapel

Wishon — Crown Valley

North Fork Kings River

PORTAL
Eastern brook 10,340
rainbow 4 acres

MIDWAY
10,650
13 acres
Rainbow

CATHEDRAL
10,750 Rainbow
32 acres

White Divide

Maxson
Lake 9,950

Crown

Basin

Ridge

Finger
Peak

Hummingbird
10,325 3 acres
Eastern brook

Kettle

RAINBOW (*Salmo gairdnerii*)

red

dark green

rose-colored band

small mouth

rose
cheeks

silvery sides
tiny scales

rose
underside

red

half of them above 11,000'. Those having favorable fishing reproduction conditions have been planted with Eastern brook or rainbow. Some golden may be taken at Chapel, Ram, and two unnamed lakes in Crown Basin.

Peaks of Le Conte Divide and Kettle Ridge range between 12,000' and 13,000' form a splendid skyline show at daybreak. At this hour the wind is low and the deep blue lake reflects the jagged peaks and entices your photographic skills. If a fat rainbow makes a slow roll off a rocky point its time for the most ardent sack warmer to forsake creature comforts and brave the frosty meadow to the ice rimmed lake.

COURTRIGHT RESERVOIR – PORTAL LAKE/WHITE DIVIDE 26.0
(via Post Corral, Big Maxom Mdw.)

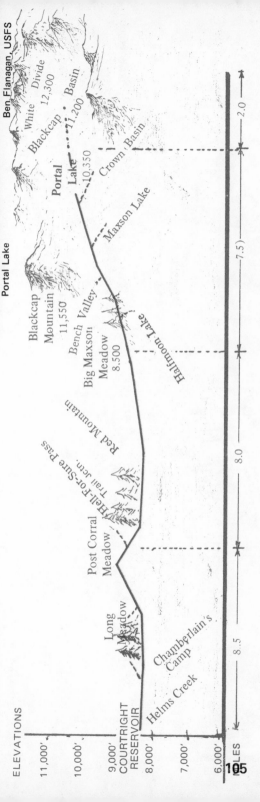

Portal Lake

Ben Flanagan, USFS

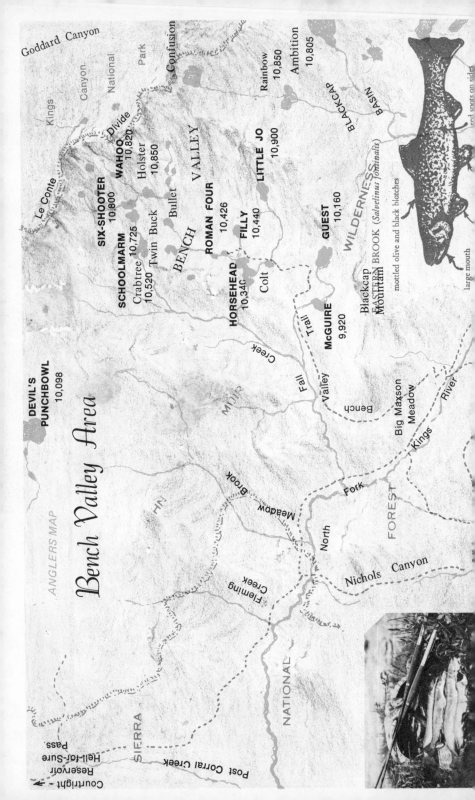

Goddard Canyon

Kings

Canyon

National

Park

Le Conte

Divide

Confusion

Rainbow
10,850

Ambition
10,805

BLACKCAP

BASIN

red spots on sides

SIX-SHOOTER
10,800

WAHOO
10,820

Holster
10,850

Bullet

Twin Buck

BENCH

VALLEY

ROMAN FOUR
10,426

LITTLE JO
10,900

FILLY
10,440

GUEST
10,160

WILDERNESS

BROOK (*Salvelinus fontinalis*)

mottled olive and black blotches

large mouth

SCHOOLMARM

Crabtree
10,520

10,725

HORSEHEAD
10,340

Colt

McGUIRE
9,920

Blackcap
FOUNTAIN
Mountain

DEVIL'S
PUNCHBOWL
10,098

Bench Valley Area

ANGLERS MAP

Creek

Creek

Fall

Trail

Valley

Bench

Big Maxson
Meadow

Kings

River

MUIR

Brook

Meadow

Fork

North

FOREST

Nichols Canyon

JMT

Fleming
Creek

NATIONAL

SIERRA

Post Corral Creek

Hell-for-Sure Pass

Courtright
Reservoir

Upper Maquire Lake, Bench Valley   Ben Flanagan, USFS

Upon examining the names of more than a score of lakes in this basin, I am convinced it was first entered by a wild-haired bunch of Fresno fishermen or Porterville packers — and however did Schoolmarm Lake get into the picture? Most of this western slope backcountry was first visited by such fellows. The nearest they ever came to "mountaineering" and backpacking was to hobble up dead-end canyons with a bag of barley looking for their stock that had moved out on them during the night.

Since those early stockmen days this country has become known as: " ...if you want to see some real pretty country, go up there along the LeConte Divide where ... "

This is a good place to cross country from lake to lake and over low divides into the next glacier scoured basin full of lakes. To get there, " ...you go down to Big Maxson Meadow on the North Fork of the Kings and turn east up Fall Creek ... "

107

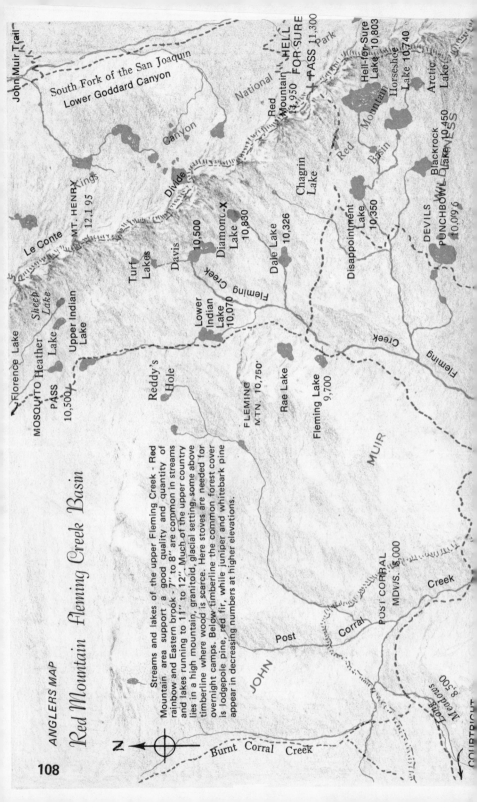

ANGLERS MAP

Red Mountain Fleming Creek Basin

Streams and lakes of the upper Fleming Creek - Red Mountain area support a good quality and quantity of rainbow and Eastern brook - 7" to 8" are common in streams and lakes running to 11" to 12". Much of the upper country lies in a high mountain, granitoid, glacial setting- some above timberline where wood is scarce. Here stoves are needed for overnight camps. Below timberline the common forest cover is lodgepole pine, red fir, while juniper and whitebark pine appear in decreasing numbers at higher elevations.

John Muir Trail

South Fork of the San Joaquin
Lower Goddard Canyon

Canyon

Kings

Divide

National

Red

Red Mountain 11,950

HELL FOR-SURE PASS 11,300

Park

Red

Mountain

Basin

Hell-for-Sure Lake 10,803

Horseshoe Lake 10,740

Arctic Lake

MT. HENRY 12,195

Le Conte

Chagrin Lake

Disappointment Lake 10,350

DEVILS PUNCHBOWL Lake 10,096

Blackrock Lake 10,450

KINGS - NESS

Turf Lakes

Davis 10,500

Diamond 10,830

Dale Lake 10,326

Florence Lake

Sheep Lake

Mosquito Heather Lake

MOSQUITO PASS 10,500

Upper Indian Lake

Lower Indian Lake 10,070

Fleming Creek

Fleming Creek

Creek

Fleming

Reddy's Hole

FLEMING MTN. 10,750'

Rae Lake

Fleming Lake 9,700

MUIR

JOHN

Post

Corral

POST CORRAL MDWS. 8,000

Creek

Burnt Corral Creek

N

Long Meadows 8,500

COURTRIGHT

108

FLORENCE LAKE · HELL-FOR-SURE PASS TR. JCTN. . . . 18.0
(via Mosquito Pass Trail)

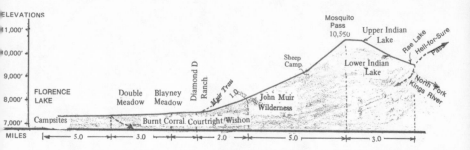

Principal interest in the Mosquite Pass Trail lies in its making accessible almost a dozen lakes in the upper Fleming Creek basin. The fishing is good in both streams and lakes. The trails are Forest Service maintained up as far as Mosquito Pass.

Between the pass and Blayney Meadows on the San Joaquin, the trail is not maintained. Karl Smith, of the Diamond D Ranch at the Meadows, reports: "It is very rough and not advised for stock, hikers can make it if they are careful. There is a problem, though, of getting across the river. The San Joaquin is very large and dangerous along here, and no bridge. Crossings can't be made until late summer when the water is down. There is no way up or down the south side of the river — too much rough stuff even for hikers."

As a vista point, Mosquito Pass is tremendous with views of the San Joaquin basin, the LeConte Divide and the Red Mountain Basin. There is good Eastern brook fishing at Heather Lake.

In early summer backpackers could better follow a northwesterly cross country route starting from just above Lower Indian Lake and proceed along a southwesterly course to a junction with the Thompson Pass Trail at the John Muir Wilderness boundary. From there the six miles to the Florence Lake campground is an easy downhill trip through lodgepole and fir country.

From Hell-For-Sure Lake, which dominates the Red Mountain Basin, the steep trail to the Pass with rocky switchbacks is a pull, but well worth it with the view of the deep walled Goddard Canyon and Emerald and McGee peaks standing guard above. Some seasons the snow stays until late into the summer in the canyon.

COURTRIGHT RESERVOIR — GODDARD CANYON BRIDGE 25.5
(via Post Corral, Fleming Lake, Hell-for-Sure Pass)

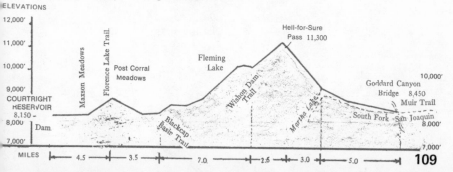

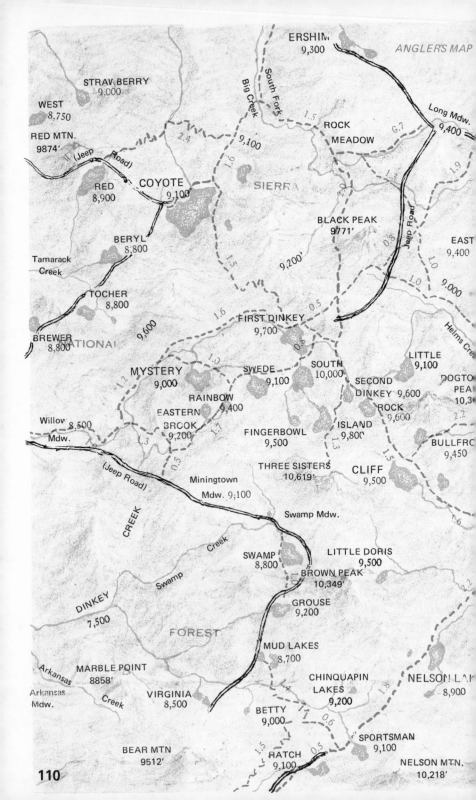

Shaver Lake - Dinkey Creek Area

The North Fork of the Kings River and its tributaries drain the region west of the LeConte Divide and north of the Main Kings River to the south. Most westerly of its important tributaries is Dinkey Creek that has its origins along the southern heights of the Foster Ridge-Black Peak highland. This eight to nine thousand foot elevation divide lies on an east-west course and continuous at higher elevations near Thompson Pass (10,230), Mt. Shinn (11,020'). Mosquito Pass (10,550'), and, Mt. Henry (12,196') in the LeConte Divide. Lying at right angles to this, the broad shouldered ridge determines the division of waters flowing north to the San Joaquin and south to the Kings.

The Dinkey Lakes lie in a horseshoe basin rimmed by Nelson Mountain, Brown Peak, Three Sisters, Black Peak, and to the west Foster Ridge. In this basin, low ridges provide an excellent setting for many lakes, ponds and streams connecting them. It is an ideal place for family camping whether they come to fish, take pictures, or just sit around the campfire.

Most of the fish here are Eastern brook that do unusually well in these meadow-lined waters. The California State Fish & Game Dept. administers the fish planting and study of angling conditions to insure a fair catch and replenishment program.

The entire Sierra west of the LeConte Divide is, except at high elevations, well forested with pine, fir, cedar, and such broadleaved trees as oak, maple, alder, and cottonwood. In suitable areas are found juniper, aspen, and laurel. There is a nice group of sequoias at McKinley Grove about five miles southeast of Dinkey Creek on the Wishon road.

The 'multiple-use' ethic administratered by the Forest Service is well illustrated in this region. Effort is made to maintain a balance between the uses of trees for lumber or shelter for wildlife and campers, between grassy meadows for stock or wildflowers for summer visitors, and between water for irrigation and power and or recreational activities,all of this within a consistent pattern with the natural environment.

At Dinkey Creek there are resorts, a pack station, and numerous campgrounds. The Forest Service has developed extensive recreational programs with similar activities at Wishon during the summer. Plans are being extended to include a year round program in this area.

Little Lake   Chuck Koons

Huntington Lake

As we view the extensive recreational activities, homes and commerical developments around Huntington Lake, it is hard to realize that it was once a secluded, pristine valley with broad meadows surrounded by deep forest - an ideal summer camp for the Yokuts/Monachi Indians who wintered in the oak tree foothills to the west.

Huntington Lake is really a man-made intrusion on the wilderness. When it was drained some years ago to effect repairs on the dam, huge quantities of obsidian arrowheads and knives were found on the floor of the old lakebed. This valley was the scene of several scores of campsites and as many more were located along tributary valleys nearby.

Through here was one of the principal trans-Sierra trade routes between the Auberry/Shaver Lake /North Fork country and Mono country, east of the Sierra. Crossing at Kaiser Pass, trails led past Florence Lake, along Piute Creek and crossed the crest at Pine Creek and Piute passes. Two trails led north and crossed at Mammoth Pass. Trail-camp evidences support the belief that the greatest traffic was the west-east routes by way of Blayney Meadows, Piute Creek or Vermillion Valley and Mono Creek with crossings at Mono, Hopkins and McGee passes. All of these were the forerunners of todays high country trails in the upper San Joaquin basin.

As notes from Muir's early travels in the Sierra read, " . . . the more rugged and inaccessibly the topography, the more surely will trails of white men, Indians, bear, sheep, etc. be found converging in the best places. One of the early Indian trails crosses the range by a nameless pass at the headwaters of the South and Middle Fork of the San Joaquin, another between the North and Middle Forks of the same river and crosses just to the south of the Minarets . . . "

Archeologists and history buffs will find much to speculate upon in reviewing the reports by the University of California groups who made extensive studies of this area. Then, from the Kaiser crest, speculate upon the culture of these simple people who had developed such a peaceful, satisfying arrangement with one another and with their wilderness.

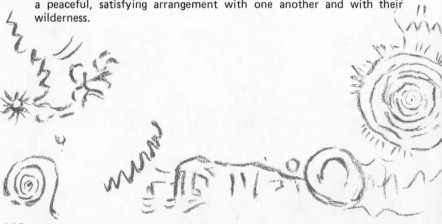

San Joaquin River Basin

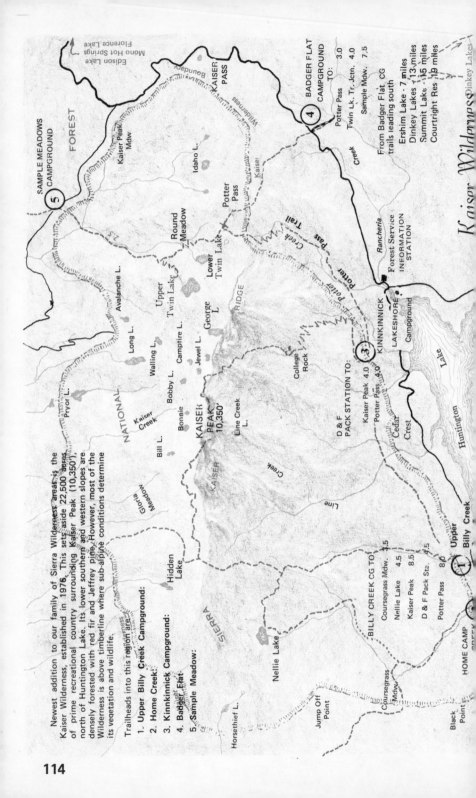

Newest addition to our family of Sierra Wilderness areas is the Kaiser Wilderness, established in 1976. This sets aside 22,500 acres of prime recreational country surrounding Kaiser Peak (10,350'), north of Huntington Lake. Its lower southern and western slopes are densely forested with red fir and Jeffrey pine. However, most of the Wilderness is above timberline where sub-alpine conditions determine its vegetation and wildlife.

Trailheads into this region are:

1. Upper Billy Creek Campground:
2. Home Creek:
3. Kinnikinnick Campground:
4. Badger Flat:
5. Sample Meadow:

SAMPLE MEADOWS
CAMPGROUND ⑤

Edison Lake
Mono Hot Springs
Florence Lake

FOREST

NATIONAL

SIERRA

KAISER PEAK 10,350'

Kaiser Peak Mdw

Idaho L.

Round Meadow

KAISER PASS

Potter Pass

Lower Twin Lake

Upper Twin Lake

Avalanche L.

Long L.

Walling L.

Pryor L.

Kaiser Creek

Bobby L.

Campfire L.

Jewel L.

George L.

Bonnie

Bill L.

Gloria Meadow

Line Creek L.

College Rock

RIDGE

KAISER

Creek

Line

Creek

Hidden Lake

Nellie Lake

Coursegrass Mdw

Horsethief L.

Jump Off Point

Black Point

HOME CAMP

Upper Billy Creek ①

BILLY CREEK CG TO:

Coursegrass Mdw.	3.5
Nellie Lake	4.5
Kaiser Peak	8.5
D & F Pack Sta.	7.5
Potter Pass	8.0

D & F PACK STATION TO:

Kaiser Peak	4.0
Potter Pass	4.0

KINNIKINNICK ③

Rancheria

Forest Service
INFORMATION STATION

LAKESHORE
Campground

Cedar Crest

Huntington

Lake

Potter Creek Trail

BADGER FLAT CAMPGROUND ④

TO:

Potter Pass	3.0
Twin Lk. Tr. Jctn.	4.0
Sample Mdw.	7.5

Kaiser Creek

From Badger Flat CG
trails leading south

Ershim Lake	7 miles
Dinkey Lakes	13 miles
Summit Lake	15 miles
Courtright Res.	19 miles

Kaiser Wilderness Dinkey Lakes

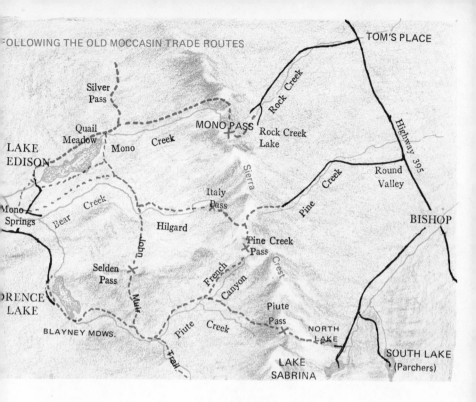

From the upper San Joaquin River basin there are several choices of trans-Sierra routes which offer a wide range of great camping experiences. It is also one of the least traveled areas in the Sierra.

The old Indian trans-Sierra routes between Huntington Lake and the Postpile/Mammoth Lakes Country, or between the Florence Lake/Lake Edison country and Mono, Pine Creek, and Piute passes to the east, provide a setting for an unusual trip for those wishing wood, water, fish, and a minimum number of people.

For those who would enjoy combining the moccasin route country with a section of "high" Sierra along the Muir Trail, consider the route suggested below between Florence Lake and South Lake.

FLORENCE LAKE — SOUTH LAKE 49.0
(via Muir Pass, Bishop Pass)

115

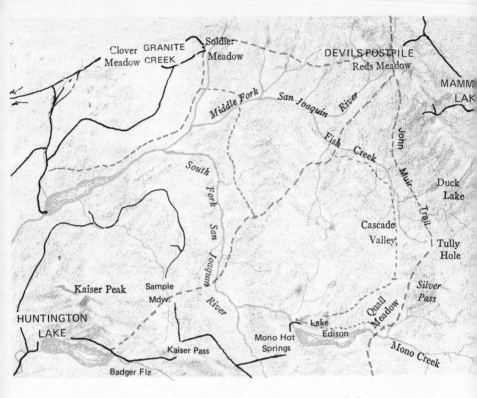

Huntington Lake - Devils Postpile

Between Huntington Lake and the Postpile, some 35 - 40 miles, lies the broad, heavily forested basins of the Middle and South Forks of the San Joaquin. It is good camping country where the climate is mild, there is an abundance of water, wood and feed for pack stock. Streams and lake fishing is good and best of all, it isn't overcrowded!

HUNTINGTON LAKE – DEVILS POSTPILE 43.5
(via Potter Pass, Sample Mdw., Fish Creek Valley)

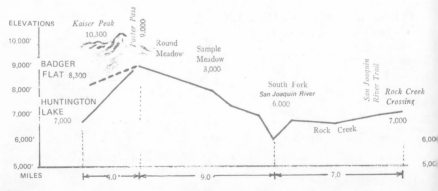

From the south, entry can be made at Badger Flat, Sample Meadow or Portal Forebay. Entry points from the north can be made at the Postpile or Mammoth Lakes. An extended trip can be made via the old San Joaquin River Trail via Heitz Meadow, Cassidy Meadow, and Miller Crossing to Soldier Meadow.

No trips across this region should overlook the great stream fishing on Fish Creek or the lovely Margaret Lakes country.

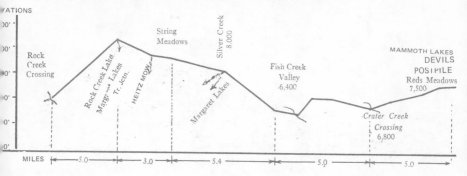

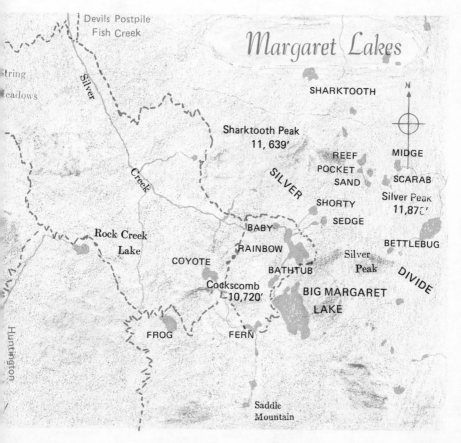

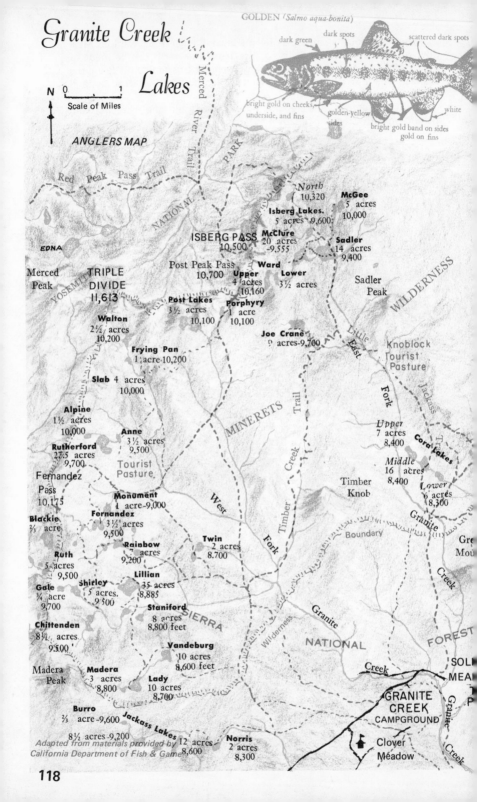

Granite Creek

Lakes

ANGLERS MAP

N

0   1
Scale of Miles

GOLDEN (*Salmo aqua-bonita*)

dark green   dark spots   scattered dark spots

bright gold on cheeks,
underside, and fins
golden-yellow
sides
bright gold band on sides
gold on fins
white

Red Peak Pass Trail

Merced River Trail

NATIONAL   PARK

YOSEMITE

EDNA

Merced
Peak

TRIPLE
DIVIDE
11,613

Walton
2½ acres
10,200

Slab 4 acres
10,000

Alpine
1½ acres
10,000

Rutherford
27.5 acres
9,700

Fernandez
Pass
10,175

Blackie
⅔ acre

Ruth
5 acres
9,500

Gale
¼ acre
9,700

Chittenden
8½ acres
9,500

Madera
Peak

Madera
3 acres
8,800

Burro
⅔ acre-9,600

North
10,320

Isberg Lakes.
5 acres 9,600

ISBERG PASS
10,500

McClure
20 acres
9,555

Post Peak Pass
10,700

Post Lakes
3½ acres
10,100

Ward

Upper
4 acres
10,160

Lower
3½ acres

Porphyry
1 acre
10,100

Frying Pan
1 acre 10,200

Joe Crane
9 acres-9,700

Anne
3½ acres
9,500

Tourist
Pasture

Monument
1 acre-9,000

Fernandez
3½ acres
9,500

Rainbow
7 acres
9,200

Twin
2 acres
8,700

Shirley
5 acres
9,500

Lillian
35 acres
8,885

Staniford
8 acres
8,800 feet

Vandeburg
10 acres
8,600 feet

Lady
10 acres
8,700

McGee
5 acres
10,000

Sadler
14 acres
9,400

Sadler
Peak

WILDERNESS

Little East Fork

Knoblock
Tourist
Pasture

Jackass

Upper
7 acres
8,400

Coral Lakes

Middle
16 acres
8,400

Lower
6 acres
8,300

Timber
Knob

Granite

Timber Creek Trail

MINERETS

West Fork

Boundary

Wilderness

Granite

SIERRA

NATIONAL

FOREST

Creek

Gre
Mou

SOL
MEA
P

GRANITE
CREEK
CAMPGROUND

Clover
Meadow

Granite Creek

Norris
2 acres
8,300

Jackass Lakes
8½ acres-9,200   12 acres
8,600

Adapted from materials provided by
California Department of Fish & Game

118

The Granite Creek-Clover Meadow country has always been considered a prime vacation area by San Joaquin Valley people. In early days, after the fruit was picked, we would go to Bass Lake and Jackass Meadows to stay with the Biglow-Jone's Cow Camp bunch. We fished, checked cattle, and engaged in some of the tallest yarn-swapping sessions until fall. Our RV was a span of grays and a buckboard wagon. Our fuel was some hay and barley to get us to the first mountain meadow. After that we lived on fish and broiled steaks. It took us five to seven days to get there and that many weeks and some frosty fall nights to get us out. Folks sure knew how to go camping then!

The country still stands high on the list of those who want real family camping and fishing in more streams and lakes then they can hike to in a dozen summers. Good roads lead in from North Fork and Bass Lake. The California Fish & Game has done a good job stocking the waters of upper Granite Creek area and the Forest Service maintains its trails. They even have a fenced tourist pasture for wrangling stock at Fernandez, Knoblock, and Soldier Meadows.

Most of the Granite Creek area lies within the Minaret Wilderness and just south of the Yosemite National Park. Vast panorama views include: to the east - the Ritter Range and Fish Valley country, to the south - the great Kaiser range, and to the north - the Triple Divide Peak, watershed of two great river systems. In between this encircling skyline lies the vast forested basins of the San Joaquin.

RAILHEADS IN THIS AREA:

1. **Jackass Meadow** - to west section Minaret Wilderness, next to Yosemite National Park.
2. **Miller Meadow** (pack station) - trails to Minaret Wilderness
3. **Clover Meadow** (Ranger Station) - trails lead to all areas upper San Joaquin
4. **Soldier Meadow** (fenced tourist pasture) - trails lead to San Joaquin and Postpile.
5. **Granite Creek Campground** - trails lead to upper East fork and Minaret Wilderness.
   Twin Island Lakes: Route follows up Isberg Pass Trail turning northeast between the Wilderness boundary and Cora Lakes. It is about 8.0 miles to the Hemlock Crossing and another 4.0 miles to Twin Island Lakes.
   Devils Postpile-Mammoth Lakes: From the roadend east of Soldier Meadow it is 3.0 miles to the old Sheep Crossing. Beyond there it is a long two mile climb up the steep east canyon wall to Snake Meadow. From there it is about 10.0 miles to Summit Meadow and another 5.0 miles to the Postpile. (See map page 84)

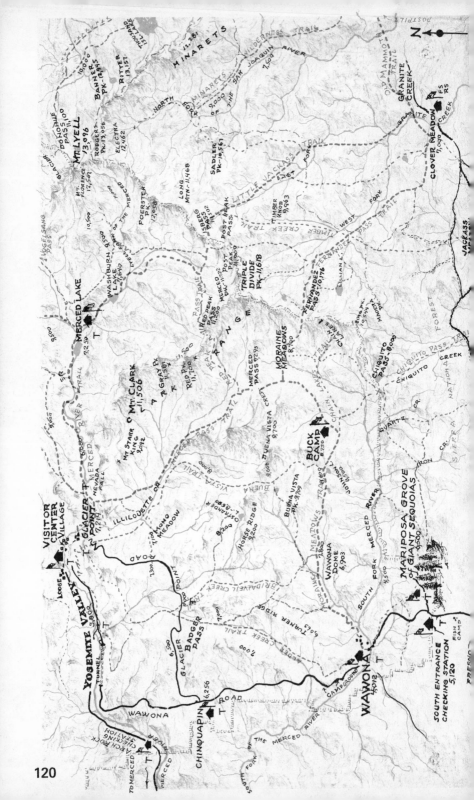

120

ell Fork Merced River

Ralph Anderson, NPS

GRANITE CREEK YOSEMITE ROUTES

There are several good routes between Granite Creek and upper San Joaquin country and Yosemite.

1. **Chiquito Pass Trail:** Starting at the Beasore Road, it follows up Chiquito Creek to the east of Quartz Mtn. (9,045'), and the Chiquito Lakes (7, 923). After crossing Chiquito Pass, a lateral trail leads northeast to the Spotted Lakes (9,000') and Chain Lakes (9,100'). The Chiquito Pass Trail continues north to a junction with the Moraine Meadows Trail. From here the trail leads west to Wawona, north down Illilouette Creek to Mono Meadows and Yosemite Valley, and east to upper Granite Creek lakes via Fernandez Pass and returns to Clover Meadow.

2. **Fernandez Pass Route:** Roadends at Norris Creek and Clover Meadow R.S. Trail lead to the western Granite Creek lakes, crosses Fernandez Pass and junctions with trails leading to Wawona or Yosemite Valley. Stream and lake fishing are excellent. There is an abundance of wood and stock pasture nearby.

    Moraine Meadows-Chain Lakes area: Near Rainbow Lake, laterals lead to the lakes south of Triple Divide Peak and Post Peak Pass (10,609'). One-half mile west of there, it joins the Isberg Pass trail.

3. **Isberg Pass:** (12.0) miles). North of the pass it junctions with trails of the Merced River to Red Peak Pass, Yosemite Valley via Merced Lake, and Tuolumne Meadows via Lyell Fork and Vogelsang.

121

Upper Merced River Basin

The upper Merced River canyon between Isberg Pass and Merced Lake is one of the most unusual and beautiful places in the Sierra. It is a broad, open, glacial carved basin flanked on the west by the towering Clark Range, and the east by the crest of peaks including Foerster, Electra, Rodgers, and Mt. Lyell.

From its eastern beginnings near Isberg Pass and Triple Divide Peak, the Merced River is a happy companion to the Merced River Trail that follows it all the way. It flows down between deep canyon walls, through tumbling cascades, quiet wooded valleys, and reaches a climax of exuberance as it plunges into space over the giant stairsteps at Nevada and Vernal falls. Subsiding in joyous melody through the appropriately named, Happy Isles, it meanders through the valley meadows of the ancient Ahwahneeches.

Along the eastern rim of this lovely canyon, the Isberg Pass Trail runs along the high shoulder of the canyon wall to the upper valley of the Lyell Fork of the Merced. A cross country trip up this canyon to its flowered meadows, timberline creeks, and sky blue glacial lakes is an alpine adventure picture framed by its majestic peaks.

The Isberg Pass Trail maintains a high profile of scenery and elevation as it junctions with the Vogelsang Pass Trail some 2.0 miles above the Merced Lake Ranger Station. From there it turns up canyon to cross Vogelsang Pass, and Tuolunme Meadows.

MERCED LAKE — ISBERG PASS 10.9
(via Lyell Fork of the Merced Trail)

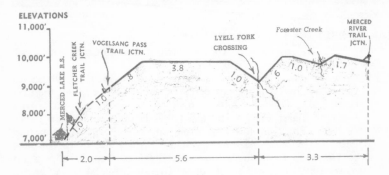

MERCED LAKE — POST PEAK PASS 16.1
(via Merced River Trail)

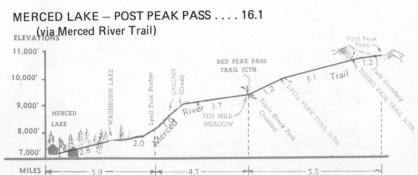

YOSEMITE VALLEY/WAWONA — DEVILS POSTPILE/MAMMOTH

TRANS-SIERRA ROUTE

WAWONA — MAMMOTH LAKES 61.0
(via Buck Camp, Fernandez Pass, Clover Meadow)

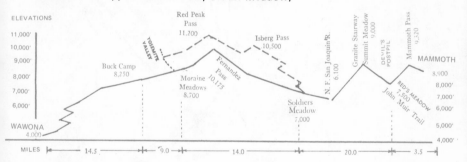

Upper San Joaquin Basin   Mammoth Crest

123

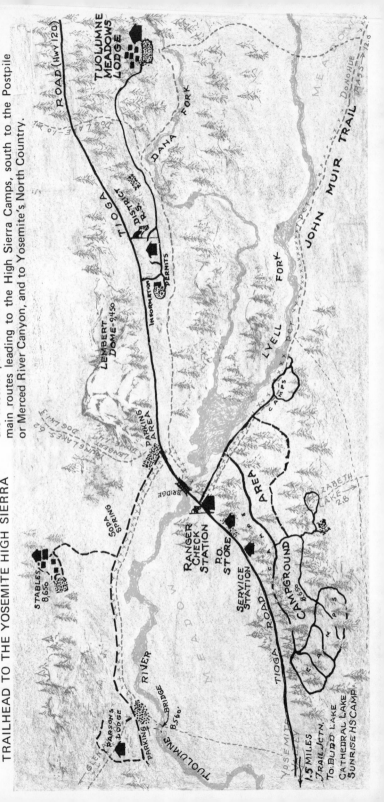

Tuolumne Meadows

TRAILHEAD TO THE YOSEMITE HIGH SIERRA

Of the several trailhead centers in Yosemite National Park, Tuolumne Meadows has always been the favorite of back country bound hikers. The Tioga Road provides access at a high elevation, saving a lot of uphill drag needed to get into the high country from trailheads in the western part of the Park. It makes an ideal departure point with main routes leading to the High Sierra Camps, south to the Postpile or Merced River Canyon, and to Yosemite's North Country.

It is a region of striking contrasts with its broad meadows surrounded by lodgepole forested slopes. Extending upward to the scattered whitebark pine, at treeline, its forest and wildlife are typical of the upper Hudsonian/Artic-Alpine zones.

It is a place of excitement and discovery by those new to the mountains. For many old timers like Naturalist Carl Sharsmith it is an extension of their home in the mountains. Season after season they return to share their experiences with others. On their days off they relax by walking to the Waterwheel Falls or, when flowers are out, going with an informal group to upper Dana Meadows. Their pleasure has been not in the distances traveled, but rather what was to be heard and seen along the way.

A FEW RECOMMENDED TRIPS

With so many lakes and interesting peaks in the Tuolumne area, it is difficult to include them all. As a starter, a few are given here. The first group requires only moderate effort that might well include younger memberes of the family. Group two is just some of the long list of backcountry treks high in quality, moderate in difficulty, that includes some cross country work and needs two to four days to really get the most out of the area visited.

GROUP ONE (Distances are from Tioga Road. Trailheads: TH:)

1. **Lembert Dome:** 2.0 miles. Moderate climb. Unusual views of Tuolumne Meadows and surrounding peaks. Never attempt a short-cut down the west slope of dome, it is very dangerous. (TH: parking area north of bridge)
2. **Dog Lake:** 1.5 miles. Very easy trip through lodgepole forest and small flowered meadows. Excellent choice to take family for picnic. (TH: parking area north of bridge)
3. **Elizabeth Lake:** 2.5 - 3 miles. Close to impressive ragged peaks. Charming meadow and forested route. (TH: back of campground)
4. **Cathedral Lakes:** 2.5 - 3 miles. Tops in High Sierra beauty amid Cathedral peaks and crests. Extensive views. Good fishing. (TH: Western end of meadow - John Muir Trail route)
5. **May Lake:** 1.0 - 2.0 miles. Easy scenic trail. Lake lies at base of Mt. Hoffman. High Sierra Camp here. (TH: three miles west of Tenaya Lake)
6. **Mt. Dana:** A moderate "walk-up" trek with extensive panorama views. (TH: Tioga Road above Dana Meadows)

GROUP TWO
(Be sure to check your route with Ranger when getting Wilderness Permit)
1. **Upper Echo Creek Basin:** Good loop trip to include Cathedral Lakes, cross country to Echo, Matthes, Nelson, and Raymond lakes. Return via Rafferty Creek or Vogelsang, Ireland lakes and Muir Trail to Tuolumne.
2. **Ireland Lake-Lyell Fork area:** A good beginners trek with some easy cross country travel to explore upper end of Lyell Fork Canyon near McClure and Lyell Glaciers.
3. **Vogelsang - Gallison Lakes:** some 15 lakes within a five mile radius in above timberline setting. Easy trails and gradual climbs most cross country routes.

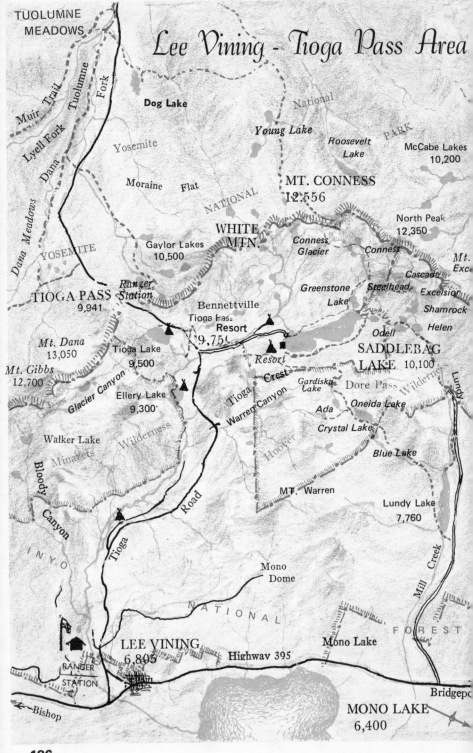

Lee Vining - Tioga Pass Area

TUOLUMNE MEADOWS

Dog Lake

Young Lake

National

PARK

Roosevelt Lake

McCabe Lakes 10,200

Muir Trail

Lyell Fork

Tuolumne Fork

Dana

Yosemite

Moraine Flat

NATIONAL

MT. CONNESS 12,556

North Peak 12,350

Dana Meadows

YOSEMITE

Gaylor Lakes 10,500

WHITE MTN.

Conness Glacier

Conness

Mt. Exc

Greenstone Lake

Steelhead

Cascade

Excelsior

TIOGA PASS 9,941

Ranger Station

Bennettville

Tioga Pass Resort 9,751

Shamrock

Helen

Mt. Dana 13,050

Tioga Lake 9,500

Resort

Odell

SADDLEBAG LAKE 10,100

Mt. Gibbs 12,700

Glacier Canyon

Ellery Lake 9,300

Crest

Tioga

Warren Canyon

Gardisky Lake

Ada

Dore Pass

Wilderness

Lundy

Oneida Lake

Walker Lake

Wilderness

Crystal Lake

Blue Lake

Minarets

Hoover

Bloody

MT. Warren

Lundy Lake 7,760

Canyon

Tioga Road

INYO

Tioga

Mono Dome

NATIONAL

Mill Creek

RANGER STATION

LEE VINING 6,805

Highway 395

Mono Lake

FOREST

Bishop

Bridgepo

MONO LAKE 6,400

Lee Vining - Tioga Pass Area

The upper LeeVining Creek basin lying west of the Saddlebag Lake road has long been by-passed for more advertised areas. Actually, its waters provide some of the finest fishing in this part of the Sierra. Its quiet seclusion from the busy Tioga Raod is a welcome surprise. The scenic crest along the White Mountain - Conness Divide includes many small ice-field-fed streams and lakes.

Several campgrounds are on the lower LeeVining Creek and valley road up to the powerhouse, or at Ellery Lake, Tioga Lake, and near Tioga Resort at the junction to the road to Saddlebag. There is a walk-in campground at Sawmill and a real 'high' country campground at Saddlebag Lake.

Tioga Resort services include supplies, meals, accommodations, gas station, and fishing information and equipment. The Saddlebag Lake Resort store has groceries and fishing supplies, a boat dock and boat rentals, some meals, and information about the area. A boat taxi is available to the upper end of the lake.

Northeast of Tioga Pass and Saddlebag Lake is the Hoover Wilderness. This area includes the headwater basins of LeeVining Creek and Mill Creek. Warren Canyon, outstanding in scenic beauty, has very little traffic.

Another recommended trip is to the Gaylor/Granite Lakes area. Trailhead for the short route to Gaylor is located at Tioga Pass Entrance Station. It is a very steep trail with splendid views south and east. There is a longer route using the Gaylor Lakes Trail about two miles east of Tuolumne on the Tioga Road. It is an easy grade that follows Gaylor Creek up to the lakes. Along the way the small groves of lodgepoles are separated by several small, flowered-decked meadows.

Saddlebag Lake   Rocky Rockwell, USFS

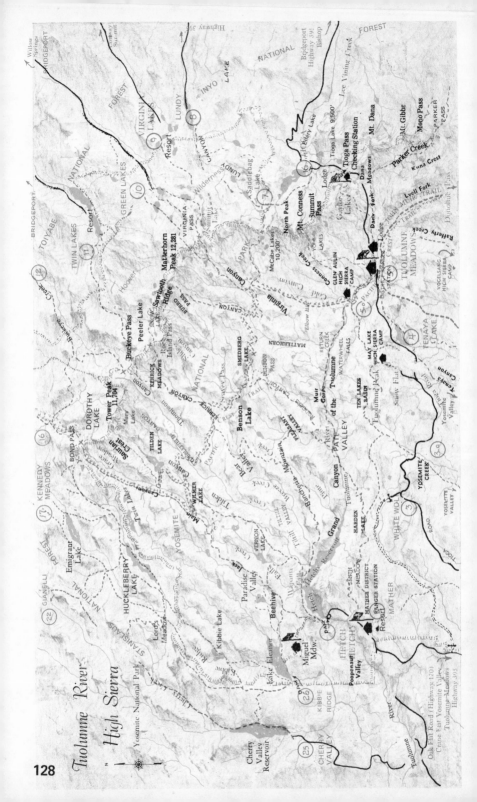

Tuolumne River
High Sierra

Yosemite National Park

128

The North Country

From its deep canyon below Hetch Hetchy to its beginnings in small rivelets along the glacial walls of Mt. Lyell, the Grand Canyon of the Tuolumne and its roaring, tumbling stream presents an everchanging spectacle of mountain grandeur. It is a region of contrasts supporting an interesting variety fo forest cover from the lower oak and chaparral valley to its wind-scarred pines and Alpine plants at timberline.

Many of Muir's early ventures into the backcountry began in the Hetch Hetchy. Here broad meadows rimmed with oaks and pines, sheer yosemite-like walls, hanging valleys and abrupt cascades and falls captivated his attention to explore the deep gorge that now bears his name. Such explorations prompted his thesis that the Yosemite region was born of glacial rather than of earthquake or faulting action.

The tributaries of the Tuolumne drain this ancient glacial basin that covers more than 600 square miles of what has become known as Yosemite's North Country. It is rimmed on the west by Kibbie Ridge, on the north by some half-dozen 8,000' to 11,000' peaks, and, on the east by the 12,000' to 13,000' Sierra Crest extending from Tower Peak to Mt. Lyell.

Here the relevancy of the past to the present environment is strikingly shown in the glacial basin of the Tuolumne. Its floor lies in a rippled pattern directing its many streams into a general southwest course to sharp confluence with the main Tuolumne River. In this vast North Country basin sierrian ice reached a depth of almost a mile in some valleys. More than 60 miles in length it overflowed its rim into the canyon surrounding it on all sides.

This land configuration discouraged early pioneer travelers and '49ers on their way to the gold fields. They turned northwest through Emigrant Basin and the tributary valleys of the Stanislaus where the country was more congenial to man and beast. The lack of extensive forest cover or minerals in the Tuolumne basin gave no encouragement to settlers, lumbermen, or prospectors.

Today much of the basin remains relatively unvisited. Its many canyons, separated by low, easily traversed ridges, provide an intimacy to camping not present in great open valleys. It is an ideal setting of moderate climate where its many streams and small lakes encourage the fisherman. The varied structural land invites cross country ventures from valley to valley and its long tributary canyons provide easy passage for loop or trans-Sierra trips.

Best entry points to the western part of the Tuolumne Country are at points (1), (2), (3), (25), and (26). Entry to the central region (including the Ten Lakes Basin) are along the Tioga Road at (3), (4), and (5). Those planning trips to the headwaters lying along the Sierra Crest between Mt. Conness and Mattherhorn Peak will find the entry points (6) to (10) most rewarding in scenic beauty. Don't overlook the secluded lake basin between Saddlebag and Lundy Canyon, or Gardisky Lake and the remote Warren Canyon. A whole season could be spent in the region lying east of the Sierra Crest between Tioga Lake and Green Lakes basin. Good camping sites are at entry points between (2) through (7).

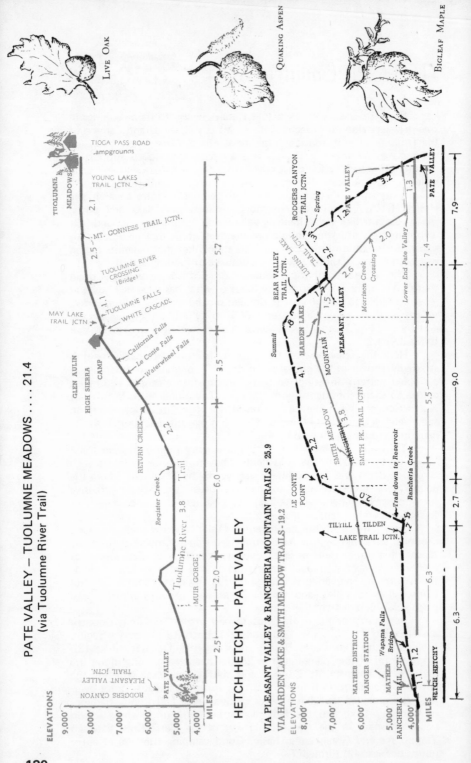

LIVE OAK

QUAKING ASPEN

BIGLEAF MAPLE

PATE VALLEY – TUOLUMNE MEADOWS 21.4
(via Tuolumne River Trail)

ELEVATIONS

9,000'
8,000'
7,000'
6,000'
5,000'
4,000'

TIOGA PASS ROAD
Campgrounds
TUOLUMNE MEADOWS

YOUNG LAKES TRAIL JCTN.

2.1

MT. CONNESS TRAIL JCTN.

2.5

TUOLUMNE RIVER CROSSING
(Bridge)

1.1

TUOLUMNE FALLS
WHITE CASCADE

MAY LAKE TRAIL JCTN.

California Falls
Le Conte Falls
Waterwheel Falls

GLEN AULIN
HIGH SIERRA CAMP

RETURN CREEK

2.2

Register Creek

Tuolumne River 3.8 Trail

MUIR GORGE

RODGERS CANYON

PATE VALLEY

PLEASANT VALLEY TRAIL JCTN.

MILES

2.5   2.0   6.0   3.5   5.7

HETCH HETCHY – PATE VALLEY

VIA PLEASANT VALLEY & RANCHERIA MOUNTAIN TRAILS – 25.9
VIA HARDEN LAKE & SMITH MEADOW TRAILS – 19.2

ELEVATIONS

8,000'
7,000'
6,000'
5,000'
4,000'

Summit

.8

BEAR VALLEY TRAIL JCTN.

HARDEN LAKE

4.1

2.2

2.2

LUKENS LAKE TRAIL JCTN.

MOUNTAIN 7

1.5

1.

.3

.3

3.2

PLEASANT VALLEY

RODGERS CANYON TRAIL JCTN.

Spring

1.2

PATE VALLEY

3.2

1.3

Morrison Creek Crossing

2.6

2.0

SMITH MEADOW

RANCHERIA 3.8

SMITH PK. TRAIL JCTN.

Lower End Pate Valley

Trail down to Reservoir

LE CONTE POINT

2.0

.5

TILTILL & TILDEN
LAKE TRAIL JCTN.

MATHER DISTRICT RANGER STATION

Wapama Falls
Bridge

MATHER TRAIL JCTN.

RANCHERIA TRAIL JCTN.

1.2

1.1

Rancheria Creek

PATE VALLEY

HETCH HETCHY

MILES

6.3   6.3   2.7   9.0   5.5   7.4   7.9

130

Grand Canyon of the Tuolumne

The Grand Canyon of the Tuolumne and its headwater tributaries tell the story of the largest of the ancient Sierra glaciers. The Yosemite High Sierra has been referred to as a living textbook on geology. It might well be added that its summary chapter is written here, where ice and running water have wrought their inevitable changes in the ancient Sierra landscape. The deceptive peaceful, flowered meadows at Tuolumne and Dana are the entry prelude to the tumultuous lower canyon to the west. The quiet and restful walks through the meadows give way near Glen Aulin to an increased personal involvement with raging torrents, leaping cascades and unbelieveably sheer canyon walls.

Below the deep, inaccessible Muir Gorge, respite is given at Pate Valley, the summer campground of the Miwok people. Numerous pictographs are found along the north edge of the meadow and oak flat. Here we leave the river where it seeks escape from the company of man in the narrow gorge leading west into the Hetch Hetchy Reservoir.

To the north and west of Pate Valley trails lead up into Rodgers Canyon, peaceful Pleasant Valley and its neighboring lakes, and over Rancheria and Tiltill Mountains. Their secluded, seldom visited streams and lakes provide good fishing and excellent camping.

To the south our trail follows up the old moccasin tracks route to the densely wooded shoulder confining Harden Lake. Here and there are remains of lateral moraines left by the glacier as it moved westward into the lower valleys before melting.

Pausing at the last overlook on the trail atop the moraine that marks the flow line, visualize the ancient Tuolumne ice field. Reflect on its magnitude, almost a mile deep in the canyon before you extending west, north and east to the horizon peaks. Too tall to be over ridden and too massive to be plucked asunder in their time, these stalwart peaks stood like ghostly sentinels above the spreading ice fields as it filled to overflowing. Its excess spilled over into the upper Merced and Tenaya canyons, past the crags of the Cathedral and Chief Tenaya peaks. To the east it flowed over the Sierra crest at Donohue, Mono, Parker, and Tioga passes and carved out the steep canyons along the eastern edge of the escarpment. Today's terminal moraines mark the limits of their flow below the glacial tarn lakes they left in their passing. The crests of these surviving peaks provide us with clues as to the nature of the ancient, pre-glacial landscape. It is believed to have been a thousand feet higher than the present crests and the erosive forces of nature carried it away down into the great Central Valley to the west.

Waterwheel Falls   Ralph Anderson, NPS, Yosemite

ALPINE WILLOW

WHITE HEATHER (Cassiope)

RED HEATHER

MATTERHORN CANYON – TUOLUMNE MEADOWS 19.3
(via Virginia & Cold Canyons, Glen Aulin)

ELEVATIONS

11,000'
10,000'
9,000'
8,000'

TUOLUMNE MEADOWS

TUOLUMNE RIVER CROSSING Bridge

MAY LAKE TRAIL

GLEN AULIN HIGH SIERRA CAM.

Bridge

Elbow Hill

McCabe Lake Trail Jctn.

McCabe Creek

VIRGINIA CANYON

Spiller Cr. Crossing

Miller Lake

MATTERHORN CANYON

4.6

1.1

5.0

2.8

1.5

2.3

2.0

MILES

7.8

KERRICK CANYON – MATTERHORN CANYON 14.7
(via Smedberg Lake, Benson Pass)

ELEVATIONS

11,000'
10,000'
9,000'
8,000'
7,000'

KERRICK CANYON TRAIL JCTN.

Seavey Pass

BENSON LAKE

RODGERS CANYON TRAIL CTNS

SMEDBERG

BENSON PASS

Wilson Creek

MATTERHORN CANYON

1.0

2.6

3.0

.6

.2

1.8

2.5

132

The route of the Pacific Crest Trail between Tuolumne Meadows and the Sonora Pass Road includes the high points of the North Country. Most of it is contained in a 7,500' to 9,500' elevation where water, forest cover, fishing, and scenery are at its best.

The Tuolumne River Trail follows along the east bank of the river for some three miles. There via a bridge it crosses and begins the steep descent into the canyon where tumbling cascades and the roaring river makes abrupt drops at Tuolumne Falls and the White Cascade near the Glen Aulin High Sierra Camp.

Leaving the Grand Canyon of the Tuolumne, the route between Glen Aulin and Virginia Canyon follows up Cold Canyon and crosses Elbow Hill summit (9,000'). Dropping down into Virginia Canyon it passes the junction to McCabe Lakes just before crossing Return Creek. The McCabe Lakes provide good fishing and very unusual views of the Sierra Crest.

A good alternative route is to cross country between McCabe and Young lakes and the Skelton and Gaylor lakes with a return to Tuolumne via the Gaylor Creek Trail. The very best in high country fishing and scenery lies along this route. (It also avoids the heavily traveled Tuolumne River and Young Lakes trails) Exits east can be made at Summit Pass and Virginia Pass leading to Virginia and Green lakes.

Between the Return Creek crossing and Jack Main Canyon the route follows an up-and-down pattern to cross a succession of streams and ridges including Virginia, Matterhorn, Kerrick, Stubblefield, and Tilden canyons. No trip through this region would be complete without including Benson Lake, gem of the North Country. Explorations to the Smedberg Lake and Rodgers/Neall lakes are most rewarding as they are unusual in scenic beauty especially with sub-alpine wild flowers in season. Hikers wishing to keep close to the Matterhorn Crest will route over Burro Pass and Snow Lake. It has many surprises in scenic beauty. (Not recommended in early season as snow packs deep in several crossings here.) Exits east can be made at Peeler Lake and Buckeye Pass to Twin Lakes and Bridgeport.

WILMER LAKE – KERRICK CANYON 9.3
(via Tildon/Kerrick Canyons)

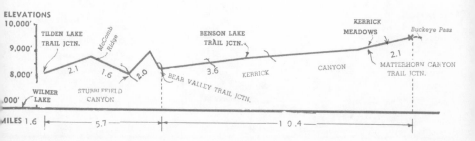

Jack Main Canyon

WILMER LAKE TO DOROTHY LAKE PASS

Upper Jack Main Canyon is an easy alternative meadow and forested valley floor between high ridges. To the east are Chittenden Peak (10,135'), Keyes Peak (11,051'), Saurian Crest (11,000), and Tower Peak (11,704'). To the north are Richardson Peak (9,845'), Haystack (9,966'), and Kendreck (10,346'). Grace Meadows is one of the real Sierra gems where in early season flowers abound in variety and profusion. An unusual side trop can be made to include Tilden and Mary lakes and Tower Peak. Return to the PCT via Tilden Canyon Creek.

Best exits southwest: Tiltill Mtn. and Tiltill Valley or via lower Jack Main Canyon to Hetch Hetchy. Northwest: Bond Pass to Emigrant Basin or Kennedy Meadows.

This is very typical up-and-down North Country containing numerous rocky basins, small lakes, scattered lodgepole groves, and much evidence of ancient glacial activity. Exits southwest to Hetch Hetchy can be made via the Bear Valley and Rancheria Mountain Trail. A very interesting alternative route includes Bear Valley, Pleasant Valley, and Pate Valley meeting the Tioga Road at White Wolf. (These high, open trails are good routes in early season to avoid high waters in the canyon.)

HETCH HETCHY — DOROTHY LAKE PASS 29.0
(via Beehive, Wilmer Lake, Grace Meadows)

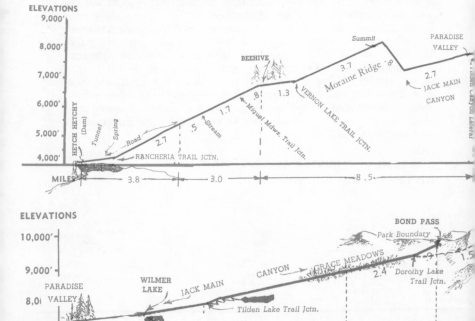

Hoover Wilderness Lakes

Rocky Rockwell, USFS

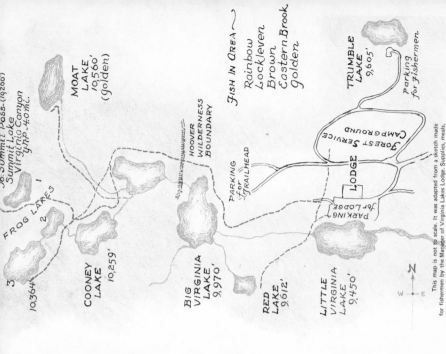

To Summit Pass - (9200')
Summit Lake
Virginia Canyon
Y.N.P. 4.0 mi.

FROG LAKES
1
2
3
10,364'

MOAT LAKE
10,560'
(golden)

COONEY LAKE
10,259'

HOOVER WILDERNESS BOUNDARY

FISH IN AREA
Rainbow
Lockleven
Brown
Eastern Brook
Golden

BIG VIRGINIA LAKE,
9,970'

PARKING for TRAILHEAD

TRUMBLE LAKE
9,605'

Parking for Fishermen

FOREST SERVICE CAMPGROUND

LODGE

PARKING for LODGE

RED LAKE
9,612'

LITTLE VIRGINIA LAKE
9,450'

N
W — E
S

This map is not to scale. It was adapted from a sketch made for fishermen by the Manager of Virginia Lakes Lodge. Supplies, meals, and accommodations are available here.

Virginia Lakes

The basin holding these lakes is a lovely area surrounded by towering crests. In this secluded valley each lake is in a pocket all its own. This beautiful, clear, crisp High Sierra setting is very accessible, even to RV's. The campgrounds are well maintained and the fishing excellent.

Loop trips from here can be made to Lundy Canyon or Green Lakes, and longer trips into Yosemite's Matterhorn and Benson Lake country.

135

Matterhorn Crest   Russ Jonnso

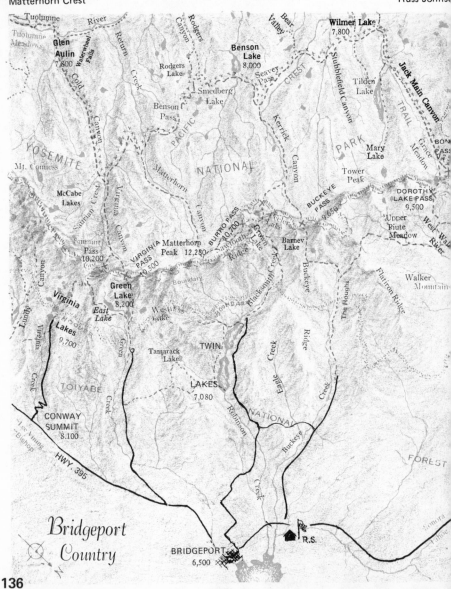

Tuolumne River

Tuolumne Meadows

Glen Aulin 7,800

Waterwheel Falls

Return Creek

Cold Canyon

Rodgers Canyon

Rodgers Lake

Benson Pass

Benson Lake 8,000

Smedberg Lake

Seavey Pass

Bear Valley

Wilmer Lake 7,800

Stubblefield Canyon

Tilden Lake

CREST

Kerrick Canyon

PACIFIC

Jack Main Canyon

TRAIL

Grace Meadow

BON PASS

YOSEMITE

Mt. Conness

NATIONAL

Matterhorn Canyon

PARK

Mary Lake

DOROTHY LAKE PASS 9,500

McCabe Lakes

Virginia Canyon

BUCKEYE PASS 9,650

Tower Peak

Upper Piute Meadow

West Walker River

Saurian Crest

Summit Pass 10,200

BUFFO PASS 10,700

Sawtooth Ridge

Crown Lake

Barnev Lake

Buckeye

Flatiron Ridge

Walker Mountain

Virginia Pass 10,500

Matterhorn Peak 12,280

Boundary

BOUNDARY

Blacksmith Creek

Buckeye Ridge

The Roughs

Virginia

Green Lake 8,200

East Lake

WESTER

Lake

Lakes 9,700

Green Creek

Tamarack Lake

TWIN

LAKES 7,080

Eagle Creek

Buckeye Creek

NATIONAL

FOREST

Virginia Creek

TOIYABE

Robinson Creek

Lee Vining Bishop

CONWAY SUMMIT 8,100

HWY. 395

Buckeye Creek

Sonora Tahoe

R.S.

Bridgeport Country

N

BRIDGEPORT 6,500

Bridgeport Country Russ Johnson

Bridgeport Valley lies in a cattle country setting looking much like western Wyoming rather than the usual California scene. Trans-Sierra travelers will find this area a happy prelude or climax to the easily traversed passes between Tioga and Sonora Pass roads. Remember spring comes late and fall sometimes arrives ahead of schedule in this region, so plan your trips accordingly into the North Country, Hoover Wilderness, or Emigrant Basin.

137

North Country Wilderness Entries

The northern terminus of the High Sierra and its north-south hiker routes includes more than good entry-exit points which, in themselves present a happy camping experience. Immediately adjacent to the many roadends leading up into valleys between Bridgeport and Pinecrest, the Forest Service maintains a large number of choice RV — camping sites. Entry point, campgrounds, supplies and pack stations are listed below.

Trailheads into this northern Sierra are shown on the map with circled numbers. Almost half of those entering the Emigrant Basin go in by way of Kennedy Meadows (17). Next in popularity are the trailheads at Gianelli Cabin (22) and Bell Meadows (24). Those seeking less crowded trails and campsites will do well to try other entry points and destinations to avoid the "over-use" conditions that tend to distract them from the wilderness experience they come to enjoy in the John-Muir Trail country.

District Ranger Station: For Wilderness permits and information —
EAST — Bridgeport, USFS Ranger Station, 4 miles north of town.
WEST — Sonora, USFS Ranger Station, 175 E. Fairview Lane
          Pinecrest, at the "Y". (30 miles east of Sonora)

CAMPGROUNDS AND FACILITIES AT ENTRY POINTS

- (6) Tioga and (7) Saddlebag — five campgrounds in general area
- (8) Lundy — undeveloped, no facilities, open area to camp
- (9) Virginia Lake — 50 sites, resort, supplies, pack station
- (10) Green Lakes — 17 sites, no accommodations or supplies
- (11) Robinson Creek — 135 sites, resorts, pack station, boating
- (12) Buckeye Creek — undeveloped, no facilities, open area to camp
- (13) Little Long Valley — undeveloped, pack station (4 mi. W. of Sonora Jctn.)
- (14) Sonora Junction — Chris Flat Campground, 3 mi. north; Opal-Obisdian, 3 miles south on Little Walker River; Sonora Bridge, 2 miles west
- (15) Leavitt Meadows 19 sites, pack station (7 mi west of Hwy 395)
- (16) Leavitt Lake — no established campsites, little or no wood.
- (17) Kennedy Meadows — 6 sites at Chipmunk Flat, resort (55 mi. E. of Sonora)
- (18) Silver Mine — three campgrounds totaling about 50 sites
- (19) Dardenelle's — four campgrounds in general area, 75 sites
    Between Dardenelles and Pinecrest there are about seven camp grounds with over 350 sites, the greater number in Pinecrest area.
- (20) Coyote Meadow — undeveloped
- (21) Waterhouse — 2 unimproved campgrounds along Herring Creek
- (22) Gianelli Cabin — no campground (15 miles E. of Pine-crest)
- (23) Crabtree Camp — unimproved camping area
- (24) Bell Meadow — Pine Valley — no campgrounds (approx. 3 mi. E. of Aspen Mdw.)
- (25) Chain Lakes — unimproved camp area at Grouse Lake
- (26) Cherry Valley — Kibbie Ridge — 10 sites, pack station (18 mi. N. of Hwy. 120)
- (1) Hetch Hetchy — no camping at the Dam. (17 miles from Hwy. 120. 7.5 miles to Mather, 9.5 miles from Mather to Hetch Hetchy) Campgrounds, accommodations, and supplies are at Evergreen and Mather, which also has a pack station.

Leavitt Meadow Dorothy Lake

This newly completed section of the Pacific Crest Trail follows on a more remote route than its previous one along the West Walker River. Its upper part includes a half dozen small lakes along Cascade Creek, Cinko Lake, the Long Lakes, Chain of Lakes, and upper Kennedy Canyon. Between there and the rim above Leavitt Lake it parallels the 10,000' crest where panoramic views of the basins to the east and north are most rewarding. There is a 3.5 mile unimproved road between the trailhead on the Sonora Pass Road and the Leavitt Lake. (No established campsites at the lake, and very little firewood.)

This section of the Pacific Crest Trail between Sonora Pass Road and the head of the West Walker River at Dorothy Lake Pass, presents an exciting venture to southbound traversers headed for Benson Lake, Matterhorn Canyon, and Tuolumne Meadows.

DOROTHY LAKE – SONORA PASS ROAD
(via Cinco Lake, Chain Lakes, Hollywood Basin, Leavitt Lake)

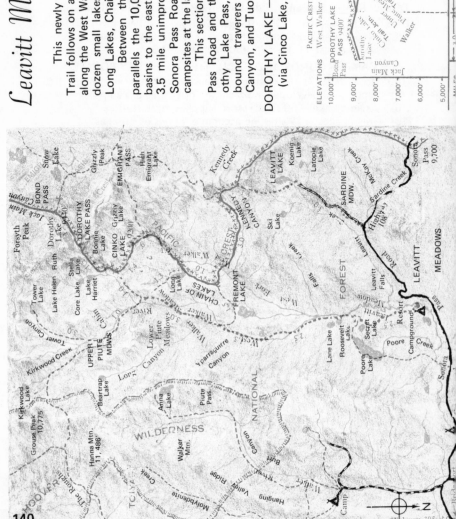

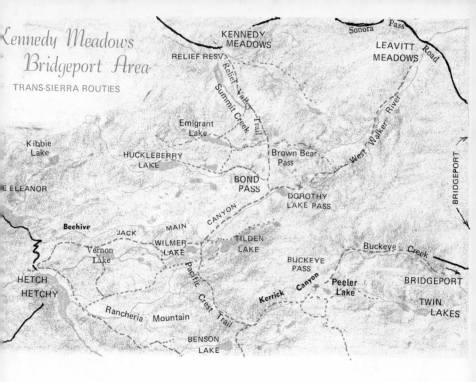

Kennedy Meadows Bridgeport Area

TRANS-SIERRA ROUTES

KENNEDY MEADOWS (Hwy 108) — BOND PASS 19.5
(via Brown Bear Pass, Summit Creek Basin)

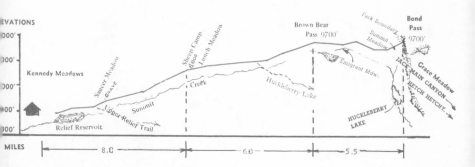

For an unusual North Country experience enter it by way of Virginia, Peeler Lake, or Dorothy Lake passes. The steep climb up these backcountry trails afford tremendous views to the east over the Bodie Hills and Sweetwater Mountains.

Crossing the Sierra here presents an intimate association with some half dozen exciting peaks, ice fields, and glaciers. Once over the crest it is practically "down hill all the way" to the Tuolumne, Tioga Road, or Hetch Hetchy destinations. For a varied trans-Sierra trip, follow the route of the early pioneers through Emigrant Basin to Kennedy Meadows or Pinecrest.

141

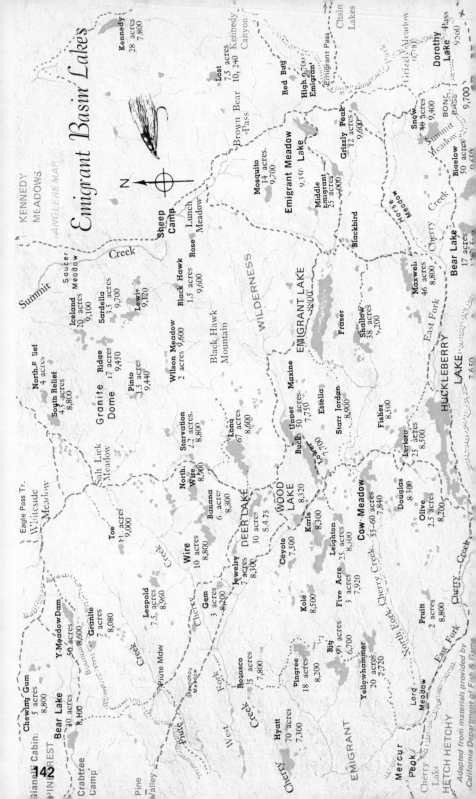

Emigrant Basin Lakes

ANGLERS MAP

142

Adapted from materials provided by California Department of Fish & Game.

Buck Lake   Eugene Rose

The waters of Emigrant Basin flow mostly northwest into the Stanislaus drainage system or southwest into the Cherry Creek-Tuolumne River basin. The country is almost a plateau in character isolated by rough crests along its eastern and southern limits, and to the north and west by the abrupt 2,000'-3,000' drop into the canyon of the Stanislaus.

Most of its lakes lie in shallow basins between 8,000' and 9,500' and are separated by low, rounded, wooded ridges. Here and there granite outcroppings present difficult trail conditions for short distances. Northeast of Summit Creek the character of the region changes from basic granite to metamorphic, volcanic materials which present exciting, colorful contrasts to the grayish-white granite structure of the Sierra bloc.

Fishing in streams and lakes is well above average in quality and quantity with Eastern brook and rainbow most common and a few golden in remote areas. In early season, bait and artificial lures resembling natural insects are preferred. Fly fishing is at its best in late summer and fall.

This colorful land is complimented by its historical past. Gold seekers and settlers coming from the East, confronted by the rugged Sierra to the north and south of here, crossed the divide by following up the West Walker River going over just north of Bond and Dorothy Lake passes. After the months of hardship across the Rockies and the dreaded Humboldt Sink, the meadows and lakes of Emigrant Basin presented them with renewed strength. Here they checked their wagons and rested the oxen, horses, and families before pushing on to the gold fields and valleys beyond. The area gave new vigor and secure passage between the deep, tortuous canyon to the north and the rugged, unhospitable, glacial-scoured terrain of Yosemite's North Country to the south.

The Emigrant Basin-Hoover Wilderness country presents a fitting climax to the John Muir Trail Country. Its more than a score of access trailheads lead into country rich in mountain splendor where travel is light and camping conditions are ideal.

143

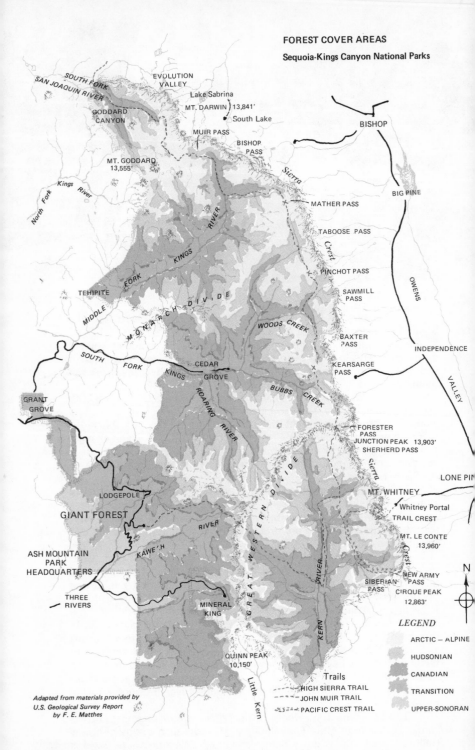

FOREST COVER AREAS

Sequoia-Kings Canyon National Parks

SOUTH FORK
SAN JOAQUIN RIVER
EVOLUTION VALLEY
GODDARD CANYON
Lake Sabrina
MT. DARWIN 13,841'
South Lake
MUIR PASS
BISHOP PASS
BISHOP
MT. GODDARD 13,555'
North Fork Kings River
Sierra
BIG PINE
MATHER PASS
KINGS FORK RIVER
TABOOSE PASS
Crest
PINCHOT PASS
SAWMILL PASS
TEHIPITE
MIDDLE
MONARCH DIVIDE
WOODS CREEK
OWENS
BAXTER PASS
INDEPENDENCE
SOUTH FORK KINGS
CEDAR GROVE
KEARSARGE PASS
VALLEY
GRANT GROVE
ROARING RIVER
BUBBS CREEK
FORESTER PASS
JUNCTION PEAK 13,903'
SHERHERD PASS
LODGEPOLE
GIANT FOREST
GREAT WESTERN DIVIDE
Sierra
LONE PINE
MT. WHITNEY
Whitney Portal
TRAIL CREST
ASH MOUNTAIN PARK HEADQUARTERS
KAWE'H
RIVER
MT. LE CONTE 13,960'
Crest
THREE RIVERS
KERN RIVER
SIBERIAN PASS
NEW ARMY PASS
CIRQUE PEAK 12,863'
MINERAL KING
N
QUINN PEAK 10,150'
Little Kern

Adapted from materials provided by
U.S. Geological Survey Report
by F. E. Matthes

LEGEND

ARCTIC – ALPINE

HUDSONIAN

CANADIAN

TRANSITION

UPPER-SONORAN

Trails
--- HIGH SIERRA TRAIL
----- JOHN MUIR TRAIL
·x··x·· PACIFIC CREST TRAIL

Sierra Life Zones

PUSSY PAWS

The east slope of the Sierra is so abrupt between the Owens' Valley floor and the crest adjacent to it that climatic conditions are not as consistent with changes in elevations as on the west. Here will be found a general intermingling, cosmopolitan arrangement of both plant and animal life except at the extreme elevations. All life as well as climatic conditions are compressed into such a limited space definite separations are seldom found.

The John Muir Trail country lies mostly in the Upper-Hudsonian and sub-Arctic to Alpine zones. The Sierra access roads and trails transcend the lower life zones. Now and then the Muir Trail will drop down into deep basins where climatic conditions will, for a short distance, support plant and animal life normally found in much lower areas. It will be helpful to newcomers to the mountains to keep in mind the above determinates of what constitutes Life Zones when trying to identify wildlife along the trail. Also, there are a few general conditions that uniformly encourage birds and animals to seek a certain area for their summer homes. Important among these are: 1) Adequate food supply, 2) Appropriate cover providing refuge from natural enemies, 3) Suitable nesting conditions, 4) Climatic conditions appropriate to their needs, and 5) Special survival abilities and habits such as migration, adaptation, and hibernation. The last conditions are especially important to such animals as deer, conys, and Alpine chipmunks; each choosing their own specialized way of survival with the change of seasons.

Most North American regions have a fairly stable weather situation developing from a typical elevation and latitude condition. The Sierran region follows this weather and life zone pattern only as it relates to southern or northern areas. A venture into the Sierra either east or west produces dramatic changes in weather, plant life, and the wildlife. Add to this the changing conditions of soil, moisture, and sunny exposure the visitor will, in the space of a few days, and sometimes in a few hours, cross as many physical life zones as he would encounter traveling several thousand miles from the southwestern Sonoran desert to the northern Canadian Arctic.

Life Zones are, in the main, a reflection of weather-belts where there is a reasonable consistancy of certain shrubs and trees suitable to the shelter and food supply for its wildlife. The average topographical gradient effect on these life zones on the Sierran west slope is about 100 feet verticle rise per horizontal mile as compared with a 1,000 foot verticle rise on the east slope. Life zone belts lie as much as 2,000 to 3,000 feet on the southern Sequoia ranges, higher than they do in northern Yosemite National Park.

Sierra Forest

The Sierra Nevada is unique in the wide variety of experiences it presents to its visitors. Its great size and topography in relation to the Pacific slope to the west and the desert basins to the east presents a continuous change of environment whether traveling on an east-west route or visiting it at its southern, central, or nothern limits. Its climate and landform differences present a setting of great variety in the type and quantity of forest cover and its attendant wildlife.

This guide does not presume to be a complete review of Sierra wildlife; only a few of the most common or unusual plants and animals most likely to be found by Sierra summer visitors are included.

On the western slope climatic and soil conditions have developed consistant type plant-belts: 1) the dry foothills supporting grasses, chaparral, and oaks, 2) the great forest region made up mostly of pines and firs, and 3) the higher Sierran plateaus and divides where soil and climatic conditions are most difficult for plant survival.

On the eastern Sierra front, ranging between 4,000' and 7,000' over a very short distance, soil and weather conditions are strikingly different. Trees are not as tall and usually grow quite scattered from one another. Vegatation may range between desert-like sagebrush flats to sub-alpine willows in the course of three to four hours walking. Even the wildlife gives a special character to the region, such as the pinon pine, extensive groups of Jeffrey pines; antelope ground squirrel, and mountain sheep.

A cross section of the Sierra in the Sequoia region reflects an elevation/climate condition comparable to changes found along the Sierra-Cascade range traveling several hundred miles from south to north. At times backcountry adventurers will experience dramatic changes in climate, forest cover, and wildlife in the matter of a few hours when traveling routes leading across the Sierra. Other routes follow deep canyons or broad plateaus for many miles before exhibiting significant zonal differences.

The maps and diagrams are not a literal definition of boundary lines, only general indications as to where changes can probably be expected. Soil conditions, moisture, exposure to sunlight, and season of the year produce many variations. Elevation alone, although significant, is not a sole definitive determinant.

The great forest of fir and pine lies on the western slope between 2,500 and 8,000 feet elevation in the Upper-Transition, Canadian, and Lower Hudsonian zones. Below that, in the Lower-Transition and Sonoran zones the predominate cover is the chaparral and broadleaved oaks and maples. Along the higher Sierran slopes lies the Upper-Canadian and Arctic-Alpine regions. Here the weather is acceptable to only the most rugged, specially adapted shrubs, trees, and flowers and even these are in limited numbers. In this high country only a few birds and animals make this their home. Some of them do so for only a few weeks during the middle summer season.

Transition Forest

Ralph Anderson, NPS, Yosemite

147

SPARROW: (White-crowned Sparrow): Distinguished from other sparrows by black and white stripes on head with one white stripe running back above bill through center of crown. Light grayish-brown on back, under-parts light. Seen near thickets in mountain meadows. Has melodious, plaintive song.

BLUEBIRD (Mountain Bluebird): Seen in flight on High Country meadows. Feeds on ground and spends considerable time perched atop a stone singing. Bright blue all over except for a lighter shade on underside. Female usually a paler hue than male.

CHICKADEE (Mountain Chickadee or Short-tailed Mountain Chickadee): His persistent, identifying call of "chick-a-dee" or plaintive "ee-chee-chee" is heard in the High Country. Found on the tiptop twig of tallest trees. Somewhat smaller than a sparrow. Top of head and throat dark; has white line over eye; cheeks and breast are also white.

JUNCO (Oregon, Thurber's, or Sierra Junco): Has quite dark "cape" over head and shoulders; underside is white. Light brown on shoulders and back, center tail feathers black, outer ones white, light-colored bill. Feeds on ground around base of trees. Seen in the High Country at treeline.

ROSY FINCH (Sierra Nevada Rosy Finch): Friendly companion of the high mountain climber. Seen in flocks feeding on snow fields or surface of a glacier. Nests in rocky cliffs along wind-swept ridges above tree line.

STELLER'S JAY: Large, flashy blue color. Noisy, raucous voice and bold, saucy habits. Lively companion in camp or along the trail. Large feathered crest on head that is dark extending to a blue-black on shoulders and wings. Light blue-gray on underparts. Larger than a robin.

WESTERN TANAGER: His flight in and out of sunlight and shadow is a thing of startling beauty. Often seen at the Mariposa Grove and on floor of Yosemite Valley. Vivid scarlet head, upper back and tail dark, wings black with yellow bars, rest of body a striking yellow. Movements slow and deliberate.

AMERICAN DIPPER ♀ (Water Ouzel): Perches on rocks in midstream, "posts" or bobs up and down when standing. Dives under water for food and propels himself with his wings when submerged. Nests at waterline or behind the spray of waterfalls. Slate-gray, shading to dark on wings and sides of head. Very stubby tail.

AUDUBON'S WARBLER: Has an unusually melodious song heard toward evening. Bluish-gray on underparts; yellow area on crown, throat, on sides near front edge of wings, and on rump. Smaller than a sparrow. Found in areas of oaks and conifers.

CLARK'S NUTCRACKER: (Clark Crow): Usually seen at tree line. Has a noisy cry, quite companionable to people. Pale gray body with dark wings, dark center on tail.

MOST COMMONLY OBSERVED ANIMALS

There are many animals active in the meadows, brush, timber and talus slopes of the High Sierra. Their shyness, with their natural colorings, makes them difficult to see. But, with a few basic identification notes and patience, the high country visitor will be well rewarded for his effort. Rest quietly on a high mountain meadow rock and look around - you might be surprised by a marmot or picket pin checking on you.

The ever-busy Chipmunks, of which there are some half dozen varieties, seem to be at home everywhere. Usually they are found off the ground in trees and brushes. In general their faces are much sharper than the Sierra Golden-mantled Ground Squirrel, somewhat similar to the chipmunk in coloration. He is distinguished by a coppery-yellow mantle, is plumper and larger, and has no stripes across his face. The ears of the chipmunk are more pointed than the golden-mantle, his movements more rapid and alert.

As high 7,500′, the California Ground Squirrel and the Gray Squirrel are numerous. From there up to timberline the Sierra Chickarees take over and are seen, or heard wherever there are groves of trees. The Belding Ground Squirrel, or "picket-pin", frequents the high mountain meadows. Its nickname is derived from its picket like stature when on watch near the opening of his burrow. They sit upright so straight and stiff by their mounds, then scurry inside when they see danger.

Evidences of the Pocket Gopher is common in the form of mounds or earth cores that are on the ground in long coils. These cores result from its activity in winter when he makes tunnels in the snow in search of food, later to be filled with its "diggings." When the snow melts the earth core rests on the surface, sometimes over rocks or old logs. The pests of our lawns at home becomes, in their woodland environs, tillers of the soil, moving many tons of dirt and providing openings for water to penetrate the surface crust down to the tree roots.

Because of its over familiarity to man, the Black Bear (or brown or cinnamon different colors belong to the same black-bear species) excites the most interest and overstays his welcome more than any other animals. The young are born in late winter while the mother is in hibernation. Sometimes they are several weeks old when the mother rouses from her hibernation sleep. She usually produces offsprings in pairs every other year. Their food selection is exceeded only by their capacity to consume it, especially during the late summer and fall when they are storing up fat for the winter. This hibernation period lasts from around the middle of December to the middle of April, depending on the severity of the winter.

Deer and the Sierra Nevada Black Bear are the two largest and most common animals. Deer, depending largely upon leaves of certain brush and trees for food, leave the high country with the first heavy snow to congregate in large bands in the lower foothills. Each spring they migrate back up the canyons, the buck with short, if any, antlers', the does, heavy with fawns, on their way to their summer mountain home.

BADGER

CHICKAREE

CHIPMUNK

CONEY

MARMOT

Other animals, seldom seen but often noted for their activities are the Yellow-haired Porcupine. His girdle marks are seen on young fir trees. When you see the boughs or bark of the young firs chewed off at the top, it is usually the work of a porcupine. The height above ground is a fair clue as to the depth of the snow when it happened.

The Sierra Pine Marten, resembling a large weasel, is extremely shy, nocturnal in habit and, therefore, seldom seen. Conies, squirrels, and chickarees know him all too well. They are his favorite food. Living in the Lodgepole Pine belt (7,000' to 11,000') he spends much of his time in trees in winter and in rock crevices during the summer.

The Coyote's presence is distinguishable by his saucy yappings at night and doglike tracks along the morning trail advising us of his wanderings. They are nocturnal hunters, very shy, and usually are running away when you see them.

In the highest meadows and slopes adjacent to the skyline crags is found the Southern Sierra Marmot. Largest of the squirrel family he is strictly a vegetarian. From its brownish-gray back (tickled with white) its coloration shades into a buff or yellow-brown on the underside. Hibernating through the long winters he makes up for it by feeding in the meadows to get over the long fast, or to be fattening up for the winter to come. The rest of the day he spends on watch or basking in the sun a top a big boulder.

The cony, or pika, a small, pale gray rodent the size of a small bush rabbit, seldom leaves his rocky home except when venturing a few yards into a meadow to feed or cut grass to store in his hay barn for winter. When other animals hibernate or migrate to escape the severe Sierra cold, the cony feeds from his "haystacks" tucked away under sheltered rocks near his burrow.

DEER

R   F
BEAR

LION

COYOTE

Dave Dunaway, USFS

Once, very common in high mountains and desert plateaus of the west, they are now quite rare. Depletion of herds was due to kills for meat by early settlers and miners. The largest factor, however, was the take-over by domestic flocks of sheep from Europe that introduced disease and overgrazed their food supply. Large numbers died of starvation. Only small remnants of early herds are now found along the high east front of the Sierra. Special areas protecting the Bighorn Sheep have been set aside, such as those near Mt. Williamson and Mt. Baxter. Specific limitations of travel are enforced in an effort to stabilize the size and well-being of their bands.

A study of the Baxter herd was made during the summer of 1976. One of the members of the team, James Elder (Univ. Michigan), observed them and, checking the effects of people on sheep, concluded: "... their general condition was excellent. They seemed to possess, like people, individualistic personalities. They were fairly tolerant of people and stock (at a distance) moving along trails but were affected adversely when camps were made near their watering holes or feeding areas. They become very nervous and alarmed by sudden movement or having people come between them and higher "escape" territory. (Mountain climbers, please note.) One-third of the hikers questioned had seen sheep. Care should be taken to avoid an increase in hiker travel, especially off the regular trail, or there could be conflict that might lose all the sheep."

The survival of what small bands we have can be credited to restrictions on people's habits when in their area. Fortunately, sheep's preference for alpine plants for food (11,000' - 14,000' levels) and their shy tendencies to seek privacy has somewhat stabilized their existence. They have survived, like the Shoshone Indians, wolverines, and the Rosy Finch, by a definite withdrawal from populated areas and have found in these sparse, Alpine Felfields a last home. Continual travel restrictions and people concern is needed in respecting the privacy of these high wilderness dwellers. The introduction of roads, ski lifts, or even improved trails would spell disaster to them.

Care Of Our Wilderness

The care of our forests and its wildlife must, at times, become a tiring, frustrating, seemingly thankless job. It must, also, be an exciting, challenging, satisfying endeavor! Long term studies are being made by concerned men of our Park and Forest service, and the California Fish & Game, such as the report below on Deer Management by Ron Bertram. With their help and our own participation, perhaps we will become less a predatory intruder and more a member of the interdependent forest community.

DEER MANAGEMENT PROGRAM

Ron Bertram, Associate Wildlife Manager - Biologist of the Fresno staff of California Fish & Game comments about the North Kings Project:

"Within the southern half of the Sierra National Forest and northern portion of Kings Canyon National Park, an ambitious deer management program, the North Kings Project, is being carried out jointly by the Forest Service, California Department of Fish and Game, National Park Service, Fresno County Sportsmen, and Fresno State University. This is a combined research and habitat management program designed to determine the reasons for the decline in deer numbers along the west slope of the Sierra and to institute management practices to reverse that decline.

Findings show that poor fawn survival, reflecting changes in range conditions caused by weather, plant succession, past overuse by livestock and deer and direct losses and degradation of habitat by reservoirs, roads and increased numbers of people are largely responsible.

Deer are desired by most mountain visitors, whether hunters or nonhunters. Since one of the main charges of the North Kings program is to devise means of coordinating deer habitat requirements with all forest management activities, all forest visitors become involved.

While backcountry travelers are appreciative of their surroundings, their activities can often be detrimental to wildlife. Most wildlife have a certain tolerance to disturbance, however, the level or degree of disturbance is important. Using deer as an example, there is a direct relationship between deer use of an area, the availability · of cover and people use. The less cover and more people use the area receives, the lower the deer use.

Meadows are key areas for deer and focal points for a variety of wildlife. Camping in or near meadows, while providing a scenic vista for the travelers, (also a colder campsite with more mosquitoes), interferes with deer use nearby. Meadows are one of the most important vegetative types in the forest to wildlife, yet comprise only a small percentage in most forested areas. Our research has shown that often 60-80 percent of newborn fawns perish shortly after birth. While it appears much of this can be related to inadequate nutrition, disturbances causing stress and abandonment of preferred habitats are also factors.

Mountain visitors should be aware of important wildlife hatitats, which becomes an educational process, and attempt to avoid conflicts. Enjoy the critters by all means, then move on so they can get about their business of making a living, too.

This is probably an appropriate forum to discuss the often misunderstood role of fire in maintaining wildlife habitats. We have been schooled that fire is bad, since it burns down trees, destroys property and kills animals. This is not the total picture. In fact, without fire or other disturbance habitat on the Sierra's west slope for mid-successional species actually deteriorates. Two examples are:

1. Tree encroachment on small meadows gradually dries them up to become forest. The diversity of vegetation and consequently wildlife decreases. Fire retards tree growth on the meadow periphery and prolongs its existance. Examples of meadow losses are evident throughout the Sierra.

2. Many forage and cover plants for deer are dependent on fire to break seed dormancy. Existing brushfields at higher elevations are usually evidence of either past fire or other disturbance such as logging. In wilderness areas and parks, fire is the only agent to replace these since direct management activities are precluded. These are reasons to support a fire management program in wilderness type areas. Without it the "naturalness' of those areas is precluded and vegetative diversity is lost.

A prime example is found near Crown Valley of the John Muir Wilderness. Permanent plots show that in the last 12 years the number of dead or decadent shrubs of mountain whitethorn, Ceanothus cordulatus, *has doubled* Ceanothus cordulatus, has doubled in one particular brushfield. This entire brush will probably be gone within the next 20 years in the absence of fire. Allowing natural fires to burn in the wilderness would increase the probability of its replacement.

Test burns under the forest canopy in locations outside the wilderness have shown that in appropriate soil types burning can increase shrub abundance from 30 or less per acre to 1,200 to 12,000 per acre after burning.

Fire history evaluation has shown that in some parts of the west slope of the Sierra fires occurred as often as every nine years. It is obvious from the vegetation response to burning that Mother Nature intended fire to have a role in the forest ecosystem. Its absence is manifested in unnautral balance within both plant and animal communities. This relationship is recognized and, gratefully, fire is being reintroduced to some park and wilderness areas. Wildlife and the forest will be the better because of it."

———————— • ————————

From the wilderness point of view, the *great predator is man.* Even though he helps where he can to reduce his impact on the wilderness, *just being there* is an adverse impact affecting mountain sheep coming down for water. Making camp in a sheltered group of trees near a meadow where water is not too distant pre-empts the nursery room of does with fawn that need such places. Even putting out *all* fires too well we have reduced broad meadows to soured mats and prevented the growth of grassy areas needed by herbiverous animals.

Putting together these diverse needs and interests have made management a very precarious occupation. Especially since man's burgeoning intrusion into the wilderness has changed the balance of nature into a balance of power and multiple use is equated with personal desire regardless of Nature.

EASTERN SIERRA PINES

The pines of the east and south slopes of the Sierra include three rather unique pines: limber, foxtail, and pinyon. They are not found normally on the west slope. High country visitors will find them in small, open groups scattered in between low ridges and even on open plateaus with little or no competition from other trees.

The *limber pine*, at maturity, reaches up to 50' - 60' with diameters up to 3' - 4'. Their thick, dark brown bark and long, spreading arms make a great photographic contrast against gray rocks and towering skylines. Its twisted, scraggly forms are seen all along the east Sierra slopes near timberline. Its limber quality is very flexible in withstanding severe storms. (Needles 1''-1¼'' long in groups of 5. Cones 3½''-10'' long.)

Refusing the sheltered life of low valleys and protected ridges, the *foxtail pine* in obstinate defiance seems to enjoy the high shoulders near windswept passes, high stormy plateaus, and shoulders of such inhospitable places as the 10-12,000' granite ridges along the Great Western Divide and Upper Kern Plateau. Standing erect they seem to challenge the elements and enjoy them at their worst. With diameter up to 3'-6' and heights of 60'-70', they attain ages of nearly 1,000 years. (Needles ¾''-1'' long in groups of 5. Cones 2½'' x 5'' long.)

The *pinyon pine* occupied a special place in the life habits of the foothill and desert Indians. The profusion of large, oily, nuts from their cones ripening in the fall determined the coming and going of early peoples as they harvested the winter food. Pinyon nuts were a basic part of their "trade goods" with other tribes.

Groves, and in places, forests of pinyon pines present a rolling gray-green carpet over the dry east Sierra foothills and far east into the Great Basin Country. (Height 8'-25' diameter up to 12''-15''. Cones to 3'' almost round. Needles - only pine having single needle.)

Foxtail Pine at Lone Pine Lake   Rocky Rockwell, USFS

IDENTIFYING THE MOST COMMON CONE-BEARING TREES

First examine the foliage and compare it with the sketches below in Chart A. Then refer to the groups in Chart B where the different conifers are listed according to number of needles in a sheath. Using this step as a base, observe the other physical characteristics, such as the general silhouette of the tree, size of cone, texture and color of bark, etc. The eleven conifers listed below are arranged in a life zone sequence from the floor of Yosemite Valley to the timberline slopes above Vogelsang.

CHART A

GROUP I
Leaves in clusters.
Tied with sheaths
at bases.

GROUP II
Leaves singly
attached to
branches.

GROUP III
Leaves appressed
to branches.

CHART B

GROUP I
2-NEEDLE BUNDLES:
    LODGEPOLE PINE
5-NEEDLE BUNDLES:
    WHITEBARK PINE
    SUGAR PINE
3-NEEDLE BUNDLES:
    JEFFREY PINE
    PONDEROSA PINE

GROUP II
NEEDLES ARRANGED
IN ONE PLANE
ON BRANCHES:
    RED FIR
    WHITE FIR
NEEDLES GROWING
ALL AROUND
BRANCHES:
    MOUNTAIN HEMLOCK
    DOUGLAS-FIR

GROUP III
ARRANGED IN
OVERLAPPING
SEQUENCE:
    SIERRA JUNIPER
    INCENSE-CEDAR

In using Charts A and B above it will be observed that most conifers having similar needle arrangements usually live most profusely in different life zone areas, thus simplifying the problem of identification.

NAME	SILHOUETTE	CONES	BARK	NEEDLES	RESIDENCE PREFERENCE
PONDEROSA PINE	100'-180' ht. 3'-5' dia. Trunk smooth, cylindrical, with little taper until crown branches. Limbs tip upward on ends.	2¾"-5¾" long. 2"-3" dia. Oval shape, clustered near end of branches.	3"-4" thick. Surface divided into broad, shieldlike yellow plates. Surface broken into small, concave, flaky scales.	6"-11¼" long. 3 in a bundle. Deep yellow-green. Grouped in heavy, brushlike clusters at ends of branches.	3,000'-5,500' elevations. (Transition.) Very wide distribution. Most common conifer on floor of Yosemite Valley. Some approx. 8' in dia.
JEFFREY PINE	125'-175' ht. 1½'-4½' dia. Rounded top and many limbs. Large-bodied and straight.	5"-11" long. 3"-6" dia. Purplish cast.	1½"-3" thick. Reddish-brown, broken into deep plates by narrow furrows. Strong vanilla or pineapple odor.	7"-11" long. 3 in bundle. Blue-green coloring.	5,500'-8,500' elevation. (Canadian.) Some age up to 400 yrs. Becomes stunted in high, rocky areas. Seen at Glacier Point and Little Yosemite.

Tree	Form	Cone	Bark	Needles / Leaves	Range
SUGAR PINE	 150'–200' ht. 5–8' dia. Flat-topped, long sweeping branches in upper third of tree.	 12"–23" long. 2½"–5" dia. Pendent near outer ends of upper branches.	1½"–4" thick. Medium brown, deeply fissured segments tinged with red.	2½"–4" long. 5 in a bundle. Blue-green. 	4,000'–8,000' elevation. (*Transition & Canadian.*) North and east slopes of canyons. In Little Yosemite, Lost Valley, along Sunrise Creek, and on Glacier Point road.
INCENSE-CEDAR	 75'–120' ht. 2¼'–4½' dia. Crown open and irregular on mature trees. Young have smooth, conical shape.	 1"–1½" long. ½" dia. Urn-shaped when green. Sections roll back when ripe.	3"–8" thick on mature trees. Cinnamon-red, deeply fissured with soft, stringy texture. On young trees is thin, scaly, reddish-brown, flakes off easily.	 ¼"–½" scalelike leaves covering twigs in tight, overlapping sequence. Very fragrant. Rich, shiny-green coloring.	3,000'–6,000' elevation. (*Transition.*) In Yosemite Valley some are 5'–6' dia. and 125'–150' ht. Those 2'–3' dia. approx. 300 yrs. A few reach 500 yrs. Lost Valley.
DOUGLAS-FIR	 100'–175' ht. 3½'–5½' dia. Graceful, with long, sweeping branches.	 2"–4" long. 1"–1½" dia. Long, tapering, and pendent near tips.	1½"–3½" thick. Made up of thick, deep furrows. Brownish-gray on ridges. Sides of deep fissures are ash colored.	¾"–1½" long. Spiraled around branches. Needles, attached singly, are flat and glossy above and yellow-green beneath. Small branches have a plumy form. 	3,500'–6,500' elevation. (*Transition.*) Found on cool, north side of ridges. Long-lived; 3–4' dia. are 150–200 yrs. while those 4–8' dia. are 200–375 yrs. old.
WHITE FIR	 140'–180' ht. 3½'–6' dia. Very massive. Lower 1/3 clear.	3"–5" long. 1½"–2¾" dia. Erect on outer tips of limbs near top of trees. 	4"–6½" thick. Silvery on young trees. Ash-gray to deep brownish-yellow beneath. Young stems have resin blisters.	1"–3" long. Longest of any fir. Stands out from branch with a twist at its base. Green with whitish tinge. 	3,500'–8,000' elevation. (*Transition into Canadian.*) 3½'–5' dia. trees range from 275–450 yrs. old. Three unusual specimens along trail near upper end Merced Lake.
RED FIR	 125'–175' ht. 1½'–5 dia. Many with broken crowns.	5"–8" long. 2¾"–3½" dia. Stand erect near tips of branches. Purplish, edged with brown. 	2"–5" thick. Deeply fissured and divided by short, diagonal ridges. Outer scales dark red. Inner segments bright red. Surface rough.	¾"–1¼" long. Four-sided, rounded on top. Attached directly to stem. Limbs form heavy sprays in whorl formation. 	6,000'–9,000' elevation. (*Canadian.*) Trees 20"–30" dia. average 225–375 yrs. old. Found on Sunrise Trail, Snow Flat, and Glacier Point Road.
LODGEPOLE PINE	 30'–80' ht. 1'–2½' dia. Twisted trunks, often lightning scarred.	 1½"–2½" long. 1"–2" dia. Very numerous.	Very thin. Light gray and yellowish-brown. Very scaly.	1"–2½" long. 2 needles in a bundle. (Only 2-needle pine in Yosemite.) Yellowish-green, often twisted. 	6,000'–10,000' elevation. (*Canadian & Hudsonian.*) Ages 100–175 yrs. common. Tuolumne Meadows and upper Merced River Canyon

MOUNTAIN HEMLOCK	 25'-100' ht. 1-3½' dia. Limbs close to ground.	 1"-3" long. ½"-1½" dia. Abundant near top.	Young trees: thin and silvery. Mature trees: 1¼" thick, reddish-brown, deeply ridged and furrowed.	½"-¾" long. Grows spirally around branches. Appear thicker on upper side. 	7,700' on up the cool, northern slopes to timberline. Trees 18"-20" dia. and 50'-60' ht. reach ages of 180-250 yrs. Upper Lyell Fork Canyon, east wall of Lewis Creek Canyon.
SIERRA JUNIPER	 10'-30' ht. 3'-6' dia. Heavy, twisted trunk.	 ¼"-½" dia. Looks more like berry than a cone. Divided into three sections. Covered with whitish bloom. Very pungent odor.	2½"-5" thick. Reddish-brown. Long, fibrous ridges of soft bark is easily stripped from trunk.	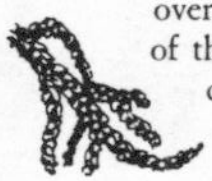 ⅛" long. Scalelike, overlapping in clusters of three, similar to incense-cedar. Gray-green.	6,500-10,000' elevation. (Canadian & Hudsonian.) On rocky hillsides. Older trees reach ages 500-1,500 yrs. High, rocky ridges near Merced Lake. Upper Lewis Creek Canyon.
WHITEBARK PINE	15'-40' ht, 15"-30" dia in sheltered areas. On open ridges a sprawling, prostrate, shrublike growth. 	 1¼"-3½" long. 1"-2" dia. Oval-shape. Pitchy, thick scales. Purplish.	⅜" thick at base to ¼" on limbs. Dark gray on mature trunk blending to whitish on smooth, outer limbs.	1¼"-2¾" long. 5 in bundle. Dark, yellow-green and thickly clustered near ends of branches. 	9,000' to timberline. (Hudsonian.) 18"-20" dia. are up to 300 yrs. old. 3½"-4" dia. may be 250 yrs. old. Vogelsang, Evelyn Lake, Tioga Pass, Ireland Ridge.

High on the tip of rock-bound pine
Where the wandering winds are free,
Above sparkling brook and blue lake's shine,
Comes the plaintive song of a Chickadee.

Where Hemlock, Juniper, and Whitebark Pine,
With trunks so twisted and stark,
Mark life's vanguard at timberline
Comes the Cony's cheerful bark.

Glacier Trails

Early studies of the landforms in North America as affected by glaciers of the ancient Ice Age have been greatly modified in recent years with respect to the Sierra. There is good evidence that neither the southern Cascades nor the Sierra were over-ridden by the vast continental glaciers. Rather, these ranges developed regional glacial activity at a much more recent time in more scattered patterns where special conditions fostered their growth.

Some ice fields and streams developed that flowed east or west as well as on the N-W and S-E patterns. Terminal moraines are found adjacent to the east face of the Sierra rampart where desert sages now flourish. Ancient valleys formed by alternate folding and stream action became subjected to glacial forces that were apt to be denied until they reached the lower melting-level elevations.

The John Muir Trail lies as near as practical adjacent to the highest eastern crest of the mountains. Its northern section includes a half-dozen passes above 10,000' elevation. Further south passes average between 11,000' and 12,000' elevation with Forester at 13,200' and Trail Crest at 13,600' near Mt. Whitney, providing unequaled panoramic vistas of the southern Sierra and nearby basins. More than 30 passes of alternate entry routes to the Muir Trail are between 10,000' and 12,000'. Numerous unnamed passes along knapsack routes exceed these elevations for the hardy mountaineer.

The full enjoyment of the Muir Trail country is enlarged as the traveler becomes involved with all its aspects. It is a land of great contrasts with its towering peaks and deep valleys. Its lush mountain meadows and alpine plateaus, its giant sequoias and its alpine willows, and its roaring torrents whose waters began in quiet glacial pools along the skyling crest.

The total range itself, a contrast with the desert-like Great Basin to the east and the fertile, fruitful Central Valley to the west. And yet, the three are as one — the towering range withdrawing the water from moisture laden clouds from the Pacific becoming the cause of both desert and fruitland lands.

Since Muir's reporting in 1894 of glacial effects on the central and southern Sierra much has been added to our knowledge about their influences on the California landscape. The largest ones, covering more than a square mile in area, are found in the northern California Cascades on the northern slopes of Mt. Shasta. Smaller ones, but equally characteristic of glacial action, are found along the Sierra crest. There, in deeply shaded north slopes, they continue their activities of "plucking" and "quarrying" great blocks of granite, then transporting them to lower elevations to eventually becoming embedded in "terminal" or "lateral" moraines or left isolated as "erratics" in some unconventional setting.

The run-off from glacial rivlets and streams become colored with the milky-white "glacial flour" as ancient, impregnable granite mountains are reduced to become the top soil of mountain meadows. In their small way they provide another type of outdoor museum display, for our study of the great forces of nature that produced the Muir Gorge, the Yosemite, and the Kings Canyon wonderlands.

GLACIERS OF THE SIERRA CREST

Mt. Lyell and its glacier
Ralph Anderson, NPS

Note the lower position on the more northern locations. In general, life zone limits agree
with this except in unusual landscape depressions or elevations.

Location on Sierra Divides and Peaks	Elevations of lower and upper margins of glaciers	Road or Trail approaches from Hwy. 395
1. SAWTOOTH RIDGE (Several)	10,600' - 11,200' (Matterhorn Peak)	BRIDGEPORT, Twin Peaks, near Matterhorn Peak
2. MT. CONNESS (Several)	11,000' - 12,000' (Tuolumne Meadows)	LEE VINING, Saddlebag Lundy
3. MT. DANA (North slope)	11,200' - 12,300' (Mono Craters)	LEE VINING, Tioga Pass Road
4. KUNA CREST Several on Kuna Pk. and Koip Peak	11,400' - 12,600' (Mono Craters)	JUNE LAKE loop road
5. MT. LYELL, Mt McClure	11,500' - 12,800' (Tuolumne Mdws. & Merced Peak0	TUOLUMNE MEADOWS Tioga Road
6. RITTER RANGE NE slope and Mineret Crest	10,500 - 12,200' (Devils Postpile)	MAMMOTH LAKES, Agnew Mdws. Devils Postpile
7. MT. ABBOT and Mt. Gabb (Several)	12,000' - 13,000' (Mt. Abbot)	TOMS PLACE, Rock Creek, Little Lake Valley
8. MT. HUMPHRIES (Several)	11,400 - 12,800' (Mt. Abbot)	BISHOP, Upper Bishop Creek Basin
9. GLACIER DIVIDE Mt. Darwin, Mt. Haeckle, Mt. Powell	11,400 - 13,800' (Mt. Goddard and Black-cap Basin)	BISHOP, Lies along north boundary Kings Canyon Nat'l. Park
10. MT. GODDARD (several along divide)	11,400 - 12,800' (Mt. Goddard)	BISHOP, west of Muir Pass on Goddard Divide
11. THE PALISADES. Mt. Bolton Brown Split Mtn., Palisade Glacier, Middle Palisade plus several others	11,200' - 13,000' (Mt. Goddard and	BIG PINE. Headwaters of Big Pine Creek

Muir reported in 1894 some 65 glaciers in the Sierra. Most
of them still exist in shaded cirques on the north side of
the higher peaks.

Above information based upon data published by California Division of Mines and Geology.

An examination of topo maps of the central and southern Sierra region show most stream courses follow along general northwest - southeast patterns rather than due west. Their final confluence with the Pacific was repeatedly delayed by ancient barriers until they found weakened ridges to break through.

	STREAM	LOCATION	Direction of General Flow	Approximate Miles of Stream flow
1.	Kern River, Little Kern, South Fork Kern Rivers	Lies east of Great Western Divide and the Greenhorn Mtns. on Kern Plateau	South	100
2.	Kaweah River	Limekin Creek & No. Fk. Kaweah tributaries	South	20
3.	So. Fk. Kings River	Bubbs Ck. to headwaters at Mather Pass	South	18
4.	Roaring River and its tributaries	Lies east of Sentinel Ridge	North	14
5.	Middle Fork Kings River	Lies east of Kettle Ridge and White Divide (Upper end above Simpson Meadow)	South	12
6.	So. Fk. San Joaquin River	Lies east of LeConte Divide, Kaiser Crest (Goddard Canyon to jct. Piute Creek)	NW	25
		North and west of Kaiser Ridge turns	SW	
7.	Mid. Fk. San Joaquin R.	East of Minarets - Ritter Crest	So. & SW	12
8.	No. Fk. San Joaquin R. and tributaries	Granite Creek & Chiquito Cr. (Triple Divide, Chiquite Ridge Basins)	South	70
9.	Merced River and Tributaries	Upper end east of Clark Range	NW	8
		Yosemite Creek Tributary (lies north of Yosemite Valley rim)	South	10
		Illilouette Creek tributary	NW	10
10.	Lyell Fk. Tuolumne River	Lies east of Cathedral Range	NW	15
11.	Main San Joaquin R.	Lies in central and west side of San Joaquin Valley between Sierra and coast ranges	North	120

ENIGMAS OF THE SIERRA

1. The difference in material it includes where, at the southern end, it is mostly glacially modified granite, at the northern end it contains large quantities of volcanic and sedimentary material.

2. A major, westward flowing stream (San Joaquin River) rising *east* of the Sierra Crest, flowing south, then west through the Sierra to the Pacific.

3. The numerous occurences of tabular (table-top) highlands said to be " . . . the remnants of a once continuous landscape of moderate relief." (Matthes). Most of these tabular summits stood much less than 1,500' above their surrounding plateaus. Their scattered, solitary existance surviving above the ice-line of glacial action preserved bits of ancient landscape for our reflection. Notable among them are:

a. Diamond Mesa (12,500') - south of Forester Pass

b. Table Mountain (13,646') - north of Milestone Mountain

c. Mt. Darwin (13,830') near two other platforms (13,841' and 13,701')

d. Dana to Blacktop Peak (½ dozen 12,500' to 13,000') Really westward sloping *platforms* with abrupt east escarpments.

Muir Crest: Looking south over *Mt. Whitney's* unglaciated *platform* top. Also abrupt east face due to *faulting* canyons separated by glacial headwalls.

Dana Crest: Looking south over Tioga-Lee Vining Canyon, Dana plateau, the east escarpment, and Owens Valley.

MONOLITHS

& DOMES

El Capitan: Height from toe to brow 3,000' with additional 500' to top of dome-shaped crown. Great blocks of granite lie at base, loosened by earthquakes.

> *Half Dome:* Mass occupies a base ¼ x ½. Summit: 4,770' above Tenaya Canyon at Mirror Lake, Form resulted from *exfoliation* rather than ice flow action Arches on dome developed from great weight of shell, glacier carried much of debris away smoothing sides in passing. Other examples not shown are Tehipite Dome and Moro Rock.

Clouds Rest: Two miles long and one mile high. One of the largest continuous fronts of bare granite in the Sierra. Other examples not shown are found on the upper Kaweah and in the Middle Fork of the Kings.

MOVING WATER AND ICE

HANGING VALLEYS: *Yosemite Falls* - 2,425' drop, and Bridalveil Falls (not shown) in Yosemite with a 620' drop. Other examples are found throughout the Sierra, such as Chagoopa Falls on the Kern.

STAIRSTEP CANYONS: *Nevada Falls* - 594' drop. Just below is Vernal Falls with a 317' drop. This occurs where there is a succession of drops of vertical fractured granite, which is caused by glaciers carrying away great slabs leaving sheer frontal faces.

photographs by Ranger Ralph Anderson, NPS

GLACIAL ACTIVITY: *Glacial Polish* - Polish caused by abrasive action of moving ice. Groves produced by hard material embedded in the bottom of the passing glacier. *Erratics* - boulders carried here from distant peaks and ridges, and left when the glacier receded.

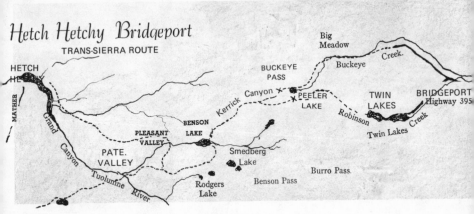

Hetch Hetchy Bridgeport
TRANS-SIERRA ROUTE

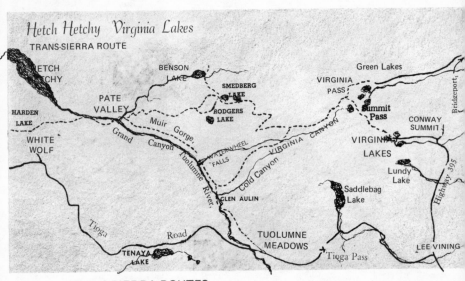

Hetch Hetchy Virginia Lakes
TRANS-SIERRA ROUTE

TRANS-SIERRA ROUTES

The planning of extended trans-Sierra or north-south trips will include many untraveled regions, where extensive forest cover will present the best in camping experiences.

1. Giant Forest/Grant Grove to Lone Pine/Independence via Whitney/Kearsarge Pass.
2. Wishon to Bishop via Monarch Divide, Grouse Meadows & South Lake.
3. Yosemite Valley/Glacier Point to Mammoth via Merced River, Isberg Pass & Soldier Meadow.
4. White Wolf or Hetch Hetchy to June Lake/Mammoth via Grand Canyon of Tuolumne and Donohue/Koip Peak passes.
5. Pinecrest to Bridgeport via Emigrant Lake, Leavitt Meadows or Pacific Crest Trail.
6. Mineral King to Emigrant Basin/Pinecrest via Cedar Grove, Tehipite Valley, Big Maxson Meadow, Huntington Lake, Clover Meadow, Tuolumne Meadows, Benson Lake, and Bond Pass.

For other Trans-Sierra routes, see pages 47, 48, 49, 115, 121, and 141.

MOCCASIN TRACKS AND PICTOGRAPHS

The pictographs left on the granite boulders and cliffs in the Sierra are fading away. The moccasin tracks up the long valleys and over the rugged passes, though faint for a time, are beginning to reappear as those who love the high country follow the old trails. These trails the Indians made by trading goods and by social contact in trans-Sierra intertribal relations.

Indians of the western foothills in general did not pilgrimmage into the great Central Valley or along the north and south route to any great extent. All along the west slope of the Sierra the repeated evidences of winter village sites, summer encampments, and trails through the mountains support this. In the short summer season it is likely most contacts were made on a reciprocal basis with communial type meetings in the high mountains.

They were not a warlike people. Their relationships became more like traders or cousins who look forward periodically to family reunions. There are numerous stories of their visits which lasted for a year or two on the other side before returning home. Studies in language of the Owens Valley and the San Joaquin Valley peoples indicate a strong similarity in words describing such relationships. Also their similarity in general social customs was quite evident. Possibly, their need of one another in both economic and social affairs had developed this intertribal arrangement and consistant peaceful interchange.

When they migrated to this western region from the east they may have brought along with them the practice of their tribal ancestors. They had intertribal relationships to avoid war and for mutual defense against larger more hostile neighboring tribes. On cases of agressiveness they would join up and if necessary move to a new region rather than adapt the "stand and fight until annihilation" posture. It has long been accepted that our southwest desert Shoshones and people of this region orginally dwelt in lands far east of the Rockies.

Even in their relationship to our early pioneers, this posture was assumed, contrary to lusty novels and Hollywood productions. They did not group for warfare activities against the whites but rather carried on what well might have been expected, a normal adherence to their life style in such actions. Their attacks upon wagon trains and settlers were primarily the normal Indian practice of securing food, supplies etc. by the method of direct appropriation. These forays were conducted by individuals or very small groups who slipped in at night to take what they wanted and picked off a stray cow or horse lagging on the long wagon train trips.

Retalitory measures on the part of the pioneers with troops and gunfire were not really battles but more a retribution to get even. As a consequence, such a pursuit of the Indians into the mountains was the discovery of the Yosemite by the Mariposa Battalion and many of the other high country valleys that had under the Spanish remained *terra incognito,* unexplored. It was referred to by the Spanish and our early argonauts only as the Sierra Nevada - the Snowy Range. It remained for todays cross country backpackers seeking out the wonders of the high country to reestablish again the ways of travel of the moccasin tracks.

165

Care Of Our Wilderness

— Ron Cron, Seasonal Park Ranger, Sequoia-Kings Canyon
National Park & Death Valley National Monument

"I appreciate this chance to remind users of the wilderness that we must be constantly aware of our surroundings while visiting the backcountry; the wildlife, the plants, air, land, and water.

The mountain ethic is basically common sense rules. All you have to do is think. After all, with no TV, radio, movies in the backcountry, what else is there to do?

With resource managers and scientists disagreeing on just what is or isn't polluted water, we, the public can nevertheless do our part in keeping backcountry waters free from foreign materials. Contrary to what commercials on TV say, a beautiful waterfall or stream or lake is *not* the place to wash your hair; or wash anything for that matter. All types of cleaners should be kept well away from any water source.

While discussing water protection, a word to the fisherman. Trout in the Park are not scavengers. Fish entrails as well as any discarded food items will not be eaten. Fish must *not* be cleaned in waterways nor should food scrapings or leftovers be discarded into any streams or lakes.

When you see a pack train on the trail coming up to you, try to realize that these animals are very simple-minded. The only thing you're going to accomplish by not getting off the trail and being quiet is to possibly scare the wits out of the animal and have your new backpack wrapped around the ears of a very upset cowboy. No telling what will happen to you.

Switchbacks were built, at great effort and expense, to ease the pain of going down steep terrain as well as hiking up. So ease the pain and follow the trail, don't cross-cut switchbacks.

Smokey Bear has been alive and well in this country for forty years and has done a great job in educating us of the dangers and care of wildfire. Care of fire, is not building one when you don't need it. It's not making a fire in a 10,000' basin when you can count the trees on one hand. It's not burning a hole in a grassy area that may take twenty to fifty years to recover. It's not blackening rocks or stinking your clothes or having to carry that heavy axe or saw. What *not* having a fire is, is clean cooking gear, faster meals, and most important, discovering the night. Look at the night, the stars, the mountains, and listen to the sounds. Getting involved in where you are in not having a fire.

To all you would-be Kit Carsons and John Fremonts, in case you haven't noticed, trails have already been blazed across the Sierra. Just admit that you were born in the wrong century and quit building rock ducs, cairns, and shelters all over the mountains.

Even though someone most likely has been there before you, if the area looks natural and untouched, you can imagine yourself the first human there. So explore. Have a little adventure, fall in the creek, get your fingernails dirty. For that matter, sit in the dirt — it won't hurt you. Mother Nature is not a bad lady. She's not out to get you. And, like a good lady, treat her with respect and you'll receive her goodness many times over."

166

WHY WILDERNESS

A Message from Carl Martin of the Sierra National Forest staff.

"Much of the Sierra National Forest lies within unroaded lands that are not designated or classified as wilderness, but are wilderness in character. This unroaded backcountry offers opportunities for backpacking, riding horses, fishing, hunting, and camping. Many lakes, streams, and meadows cover the area and attract recreationists each year and offers opportunities for a degree of solitude that is not found in more popular places.

Areas of concentrated use where resource impacts were not tolerable have been eliminated in most cases and are being eased out as soon as they can be identified. The growth of enviromental awareness during the past decade has aided in minimizing adverse impacts and maximizing recreational use.

The role played by the public as users of our backcountry and Wilderness Areas will determine the success or failure of these resources for us and those generations to follow. Obtaining your Wilderness Permit with the Supplemental Regulations that apply to areas you visit is the beginning of your commitment to the future. Understanding, and practicing protection will assure you and the future of a continuing recreation resource."

CARL MARTIN
Wilderness Assistant
Pineridge Ranger District,
Shaver Lake, CA

YOUR WILDERNESS PERMIT

1. They are required of all day hiking and overnight camping in any backcountry areas in National Forest, National Parks and Wilderness Areas. Regulations vary according to the needs of the area you may visit.
2. Your permit is valid in any continguous National Forest or Primitive Area. It is a one-time permit, free, good only for the specific dates and places listed.
3. Get your permit through the agency administrating the area where you plant to start your trip.
4. Many areas work in a quota system, only a certain number can enter a particular areas on a given day. Other areas where travel is light, do not have quotas.

WHY PERMITS?

1. Reduce visitor impact in critical areas.
2. Improve user behavior through informal contact between Rangers and visitors.
3. Collect data to assist in planning improved services for another season.
4. Improve information and rescue services in case of emergencies. (Someone knows where you are in case you don't come out when expected, or someone needs to reach you.)

167

"I am about to venture on a backcountry trip. Are Parks, Forests, Wilderness Areas, alike in their regulations? If not, what is the difference? What's expected of me?" — a fair question by any hiker or camper.

THE NATIONAL PARK SERVICE

(Administered by the Department of the Interior) Includes more than 270 Natural, Historical, and Recreational areas of national significance. It's aim is "to promote and regulate the use of these areas to conserve the scenery and the natural and historical objects and the wildlife therein — by such means as will leave them unimpaired for the enjoyment of future generations."

There is no lumbering, public grazing, or hunting. All commercial activities are kept at a minimum and must be related to essential visitor needs. Parks are basically not recreation centers. They are Nature's Museums of the great out-of-doors, or centers for the preservation of places of importance in history of our country. Your dog must be under physical control at all times and under no circumstances are they allowed on any backcountry trails. If traveling from a National Forest into a National Park remember — no guns, or dogs across the boundary!

THE NATIONAL FOREST SYSTEM

(Administered by the Department of Agriculture) Includes 187 million acres in 154 National Forests. Its multiple use and sustained yield programs relate to the management of activities such as lumbering, grazing, mining, wildlife preservation, and general recreational programs.

In the later respect, it provides some 6,000 campgrounds, and Visitor Information services. In the Sierra National Forests you may encounter lumber trucks, stock moving up to high grazing meadows, fishermen and hunters, resorts, and extensive recreational centers such as Mammoth Lakes. In most areas your dog (under control) is a welcome member of your family group.

WILDERNESS AREAS

These are found with or adjacent to both National Forests and National Parks. Very special regulations apply to them. Basically, they aim to reduce to a minimum the impact of man on the environment and its attendant wildlife. No new trails or roads, existing ones are not expanded or improved above pre-Wilderness status conditions. Contact the Ranger Station appropriate to the area you plan to visit for its special regulations. They may vary somewhat from area to area or season to season. Large scale maps showing important features and use conditions are available at Ranger offices nearest each area.

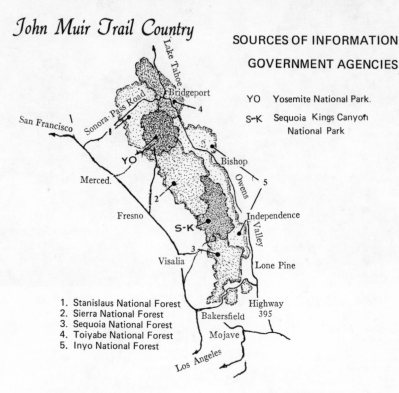

John Muir Trail Country

YO   Yosemite National Park.

S-K   Sequoia Kings Canyon
        National Park

1. Stanislaus National Forest
2. Sierra National Forest
3. Sequoia National Forest
4. Toiyabe National Forest
5. Inyo National Forest

Superintendent
Sequoia-Kings Canyon National Parks
Ash Mountain, Sequoia, CA, 93262

Superintendent
Yosemite National Park
Yosemite, CA, 95389

Region Hdqrs. National Forests
630 Sansome Street
San Francisco, Ca, 94111

Topographical Maps
Director, USGS
Federal Center
Denver, Colo., 80225

California State Fish & Game Dept.
9th & O Sts.
Sacramento, CA, 95814

Eastern High Sierra Packers Assn.
Box 147
Bishop, CA, 93514

High Sierra Packers Assn.
P.O. Box 123
Madera, CA, 93637

Interagency Visitor Information Center
Lone Pine   for Owens Valley
CA, 93545

Cannell Meadow Ranger Station
Sequoia National Forest
P.O. Box 5, Kernville, CA, 93238

Mt. Whitney Ranger Station
Inyo National Forest
P.O. Box 8, Lone Pine, CA, 93545

Forest Supervisor
Sequoia National Forest
900 W. Grand Ave.
Porterville, Ca, 93257

Forest Supervisor
Inyo National Forest
789 N. Main Street
Bishop, CA, 93514

Forest Supervisor
Sierra National Forest
Fresno, CA, 93721

Forest Supervisor
Stanislaus National Forest
175 S. Fairview Lane
Sonora, CA, 95370

Toiyabe National Forest
Bridgeport Ranger Station
Bridgeport, CA, 93517

Recreational Wilderness Information
Pineridge Ranger Station
Shaver Lake, CA, 93657

169

999 Exciting Places to Go   Eugene Rose

Murro Blanco   Eugene Rose

Bear Creek   Eugene Rose

In Appreciation . . .

WHITE HEATHER
(*Cassiope*)

The writers would like to extend their appreciation to the following people who have given their time and assistance in checking maps, providing photographs, and other interpretative materials making this book as accurate, up-to-date, and useful as possible:-

SEQUOIA NATIONAL PARK:
John Palmer, Chief Park Interpreter
Richard Burns, Assistant Chief Park Interpreter
Jack Lewis, Maintenance Supervisor, Sequoia District
Ron Cron, Backcountry Ranger, Seasonal

YOSEMITE NATIONAL PARK:
Leonard McKenzie, Chief Park Interpreter
Herb Ewing, District Ranger, Tuolumne Meadows
Ronald Mackie, Park Ranger & Backcountry Unit Manager

INYO NATIONAL FOREST:
Robert L. Rice, Forest Supervisor
Edwin C. (Rocky) Rockwell, Forest Photographer
Ernest DeGraf, Resource Officer, Lone Pine Ranger Dist.

SIERRA NATIONAL FOREST:
Ben Flanagan, Range Technician, Kings River Ranger Dist.
Carl Martin, Wilderness Assistant, Pineridge Ranger Dist.
Butch Jones, Supervisory Forest Technician, Minarets R. Dist.

STANISLAUS NATIONAL FOREST:
Tom Beck, Resource Officer, Sonora Ranger District

TOIYABE NATIONAL FOREST:
Rudolph H. Robles, Forester, Bridgeport Ranger District

CALIFORNIA FISH & GAME:
Ron Bertram, Biologist, Fresno District Office
Chuck Koons, Shaver Lake

SPECIAL PHOTOGRAPHY CREDITS

Special thanks to Eugene Rose of the Fresno Bee and Alfred Mikesell for their assistance regarding photography, as well as to the family of Orland Bartholomew for their permission to use his photograph on page 15.

Front Cover: Banner Peak - Thousand Island Lake, Rocky Rockwell,
Back Cover: White Heather (Cassiope), Rocky Rockwell
> Muir's quest in life sought the secrets of the rocks in close harmony with the beauty of the wilderness. His gentleness of spirit was reflected in his love of flowers, of which the white heather (cassiope) was his favorite.

Inside Back Cover: Authors, Eugene Rose
Inside Front Cover Montage Photographs: Russ Johnson, Rocky Rockwell, and the authors.